THINK
IT
BE
IT

THE POWER OF A POSITIVE MINDSET

BY

M.A. GLENIS

Acknowledgments

Thank you to my mother, sisters, and brother– who often lent me their light, strength, and laughter in my moments of darkness.

Thank you to my children, who are so much more than anything I could have imagined. I love you beyond time and the limits of existence.

Thank you to my dad, who gave me my smile. You were taken way too soon. You are deeply missed, Baba.

Thank you to my husband. I see you in our daughter's beautiful eyes and our son's humble genius. You are still a part of every day.

Thank you to S.J.S. & M.M. & C.B. for inspiring positivity always.

Thank you to L.S. for being my constant for 30 years; I remain forever grateful.

CONTENTS

Introduction 5

Chapter One: The Basics 11

Chapter Two: Embracing Self-Identity 21

Chapter Three: I Believe – Cultivating Belief 25

Chapter Four: I Feel– Connecting with Emotions 29

Chapter Five: I Speak – The Power of Words 35

Chapter Six: I Hear – Listening 40

Chapter Seven: I Write – The Power of the Pen 45

Chapter Eight: Wealth and Abundance Mindset 49

Chapter Nine: Cultivating Self-Love 58

Chapter Ten: Attracting Love 65

Chapter Eleven: Healthy Eating 72

Chapter Twelve: Ensuring a Good Night's Sleep 81

Chapter Thirteen: Opportunities 85

Chapter Fourteen: The Transformative Power of Gratitude 90

Chapter Fifteen: Authenticity 95

Chapter Sixteen: Laugh About It 99

Conclusion 102

Bonus: Additional Affirmations 107

Write Your Own Affirmations 121

Introduction

In this colorful tapestry we call life, it is the *ordinary* threads that are woven together, which create extraordinary stories. These ordinary moments end up meaning so much more.

I am not here as someone who was given a perfect script for life but as a regular woman who faced the challenges of cancer multiple times, the loss of a spouse, and the daunting task of raising children alone.

Over the hardest years, I was often asked, "How do you do it all?" In the past, I used to answer, "I had no choice." But, over time, I realized I could do it all because I was making CHOICES. A constant series of deliberate choices at each impasse propelled me forward and allowed me to do what needed to be done.

Today, I want to share the wisdom I gained through these experiences – the profound realization that everyday people, like you and me, can conquer the insurmountable. In the following pages, you will discover different ways that maintaining a positive mindset can help you change your well-being and transform all aspects of your life. Changing your mindset starts with a series of small choices that lead to a series of deliberate actions. This combination of choices and actions will help you **retrain your brain** to see things in a different light.

If I can change my cynical outlook, anyone can do it! I was the QUEEN of skeptics, eye-rolling at anything that smelled of "new age" fluff. Frankly, I still call BS on some ideas that are floating around. Yet, here I am, inviting you to sift through these ideas for yourself. Embrace what resonates and move on from what doesn't.

I fell into a rabbit hole of research and reading and found correlations that I couldn't ignore. On the flip side, many things I looked into just didn't fit into my life, perspective, or belief system. I am here to tell you that it's okay; not everything is for everyone, and yes, *you can pick and choose* – because I did, and I still achieved the results I desired.

The simple act of tweaking my mindset and sprinkling a little positivity into my daily brew did wonders. I started feeling better and looking better. I blossomed into a version of myself I adore, brimming with happiness that once seemed a far-off dream. There are times I don't even recognize this happier person I have become, but I LOVE HER – this NEW ME – so much. A smile is my first task each morning, setting the stage for a day drenched in gratitude. This newfound joy? It's become a bit contagious, and I'm all in for spreading it.

Life as we know it can be a rollercoaster of highs and lows. We often find ourselves questioning whether there's more to life than the day-to-day grind of work, responsibility, and all the stressors surrounding us. We wonder whether we can achieve our dreams and aspirations and find true happiness and fulfillment. It can sometimes seem that overwhelming hardships are hurled at us way too fast and way too often.

Yet, what truly defines our journey is how we steer through these twists and turns. It's not about avoiding challenges and hurdles or seeing them as dead ends but about embracing them with a positive outlook. Instead of seeing obstacles as roadblocks, I began to view them as steppingstones to getting to where I needed to be.

Everyone can cultivate a positive mindset. It is not a characteristic reserved for a select few; it's a choice accessible to all, turning everyday challenges into opportunities for growth. When faced with challenges or difficulties, the ability to find a positive aspect in the situation *can* change the outcome. It will most certainly change how we *feel* about the outcome. This is not to say that having a positive mindset is easy, but it is a skill that can be developed with practice.

By reframing negative thoughts, focusing on gratitude, and seeking positive experiences, we can train our minds to approach life more optimistically. Ultimately, the power to shape our mindset lies within us, and we can transform our lives by choosing to see the good in almost every situation.

An important part of reframing our negative thoughts comes in the form of humor. Many times, the challenges we face day to day really can seem daunting. It is natural to experience a range of emotions along the way. Tears and sadness may accompany life's difficulties, but humor can play a decisive role in helping us cope. In fact, laughter can be a potent elixir for the soul, helping us find solace and strength in the face of hardships. Just think about the times in your life when you were at your lowest. Did you have friends who would try to cheer you up by cracking jokes to make it sound like it wasn't all that bad? Maybe you're just like me, using twisted humor to diffuse the tension of complex situations. Perhaps it's even in your own arsenal of coping mechanisms – joking about difficult situations at hand! That's because it's easier on the mind to make *light* of a problem that's difficult to deal with than if we *only* see the seriousness of the situation.

Even in the darkest of times, moments of levity and laughter have reminded me that joy can coexist with sorrow. It's the ability to find humor in the mundane, to laugh in the face of challenges, which adds a touch of sparkle to our lives. So, the next time life throws you a curveball, try to find humor in the situation. Crack a joke, watch a funny movie, or laugh with friends and family. Humor can help you face your challenges with grace. Try it! You might find that laughter truly is the best medicine. And yes, you might even find a bit of my humor throughout this book – it's a big part of my big personality!

I personally have navigated the gnarliest moments of my life by finding humor in adversity. To lighten the heavy load of my past experiences, I often tell my traumatizing backstory like it was a bit in some stand-up comedy routine. This method is a strategic way to process and share my story, making it less burdensome for me and anyone listening.

In these pages, we also consider the role of *faith* and belief. As we walk the path of positivity, faith can be a guiding light that illuminates the way. Whether you call it prayer (as I do), meditation, or simply connecting with a higher power, the essence remains the same – a belief in something greater than us. Faith, in whatever shape it takes for you, acts as a beacon of hope, intertwining with positivity to guide our steps.

Faith is a cornerstone of **resilience**, providing a steadfast bedrock upon which we can weather life's storms. It instills a sense of grit, empowering us to navigate challenges with grace and perseverance. For me, faith has been a constant source of strength, providing solace and support during challenging times.

Aligning with a higher power doesn't mean surrendering control but finding comfort in knowing that a force beyond our understanding is working in our favor. A benevolent force that is always rooting for us and cheering us on from the sidelines. Remember, you have the power to believe in anything you want. Whether you use the term higher power, "God" (as I do), or prefer the term "universe" (which will be used throughout this book to ensure inclusivity), your beliefs can help reform your perspective and bring positivity into your life.

We all hold the key to morphing our ordinary existence into something extraordinary. It's time to tap into that latent spark within us all.

Now, before we go too far, let me set the record straight—I'm not a professional writer, despite the evidence of this book being in your hands. Writing is not my day job. It wasn't even a hobby till I put pen to paper some weeks ago. This is not some attempt at crafting a literary masterpiece. There is no aim or expectation for accolades. *Spoiler alert!* You won't find any shockingly revolutionary or groundbreaking revelations or deep philosophical insights within these pages—no instant fixes either—no "abracadabra" or wand-waving to offer. No mysterious "secrets" are revealed. Instead, what you'll find here is what changed my life. This is simply an account of **my experiences.** I share the straightforward steps I took to shift my mindset, drawing from my learning and understanding as I did the inner and outer work to change. Maybe you want to do something similar. This is *why* I am sharing. You are probably already familiar with some of these ideas. Therefore, diving deeper into them and applying what resonates with you in your daily life shouldn't be too much of a stretch.

My intention here wasn't to paint rainbows or sprinkle glittery metaphors. Rather, I aim to share **practical tips and techniques** to help others find the **simple joys and profound happiness** that positivity can bring. I've seen tangible results in various aspects of my life. Everything started to flow a bit smoother and then a lot smoother. I began noticing a steady stream of small victories, eventually leading to significant wins. Things are just *better* for me, and I am **so happy** and fulfilled. I want this for everyone. **I wish this for you**.

Some tiny examples of what I noticed and how things started: stumbling upon a stash of cash in the pockets of coats or purses—not just loose change, significant amounts of money! Or effortlessly finding a parking spot every time. Friends surprising me with unexpected visits and showering me with gifts from afar. Opening my mail to find totally unexpected tax refunds or refunds for the overage in my mortgage escrow account. Getting more compliments and people being kinder to me in general. A letter from the airline reminding me I had an unused e-credit for a flight. Stumbling upon forgotten gift cards or vouchers while sorting through paperwork. I received discount offers, event invitations, surprise gifts arriving at my doorstep, or gift certificates to my favorite spa hiding in my inbox. Heck, I even recently won the office Super Bowl pool for multiple quarters without having a clue about football or even watching the game. Not even for the commercials!

Then there were the financial perks—I started noticing more dividend deposits popping up on my stock app screens, and my investment portfolio began to flourish. For the first time in my life, I started saving money, paying myself first each pay period, and those small amounts began to accumulate into a nest egg. Somehow, I was making better stock picks and choices. Things were looking up, and it was a welcome change.

I was paid back on a personal loan I had extended -for the first time in my life. Over the years, I had often lent money in small and large amounts to extended family and friends. Most of the time, when I loaned the money- I had no real expectation of getting it back. No one had ever paid me back before, so I didn't know what to do when it happened. Do I accept it, refuse it, donate it? I had no clue how to handle it as it was a totally new experience. It was pretty comical, as I was confused and slightly embarrassed about accepting the money back. Ultimately, I accepted it as I didn't want to disrespect the person who kept their promise. I used some of it to help someone in need, making me feel good. The person who paid me back restored my faith in people doing the right thing! Another win!

Sure, these victories might seem trivial to some, but each brought a smile and a boost to my mood. What started as occasional happy surprises soon became a constant stream of positive occurrences. Some might chalk it up to luck, coincidence, or random synchronicity, but I wasn't concerned with labels. I was grateful to be riding this wave of good fortune day in and day out. *Why* it was happening wasn't as important to me as that it **was** happening.

And the best part? This streak of good luck has kept up. It's been quite a while now, and if anything, the frequency and speed of these little synchronicities have only increased.

So, I confidently concluded that there's a direct connection between the shifts in my mindset and the results I'm experiencing—a reality I enjoy every day. It wasn't even really that hard to do. I mean, there was definitely some work involved, but the hardest part was **believing** in some of the concepts I had to explore to get here.

Something special changed *inside me* and impacted everything else in the world *outside me*. So, now let's explore that special something that already exists inside **you**!

Chapter One

The Basics

Have you ever realized that how you speak about yourself and your circumstances can completely change how you view your life and your circumstances? Think about it – when you are extremely pessimistic, do you tend to feel like everything that day is *proving* to you that **life sucks**? Or do you find it easy to be positive? The former is much more likely to be the case. This is because we have the option to either boost our positivity by being careful of the way in which we talk or to push ourselves down by being intensely negative.

This first chapter is meant to lay the groundwork. It will require of you – a *very open mind.*

Words are powerful tools that can shape our reality. Affirmations, which appear to be just simple, small sentences, are, in fact, incredibly profound. They are seeds planted in the fertile soil of our minds. When they're positive, they can influence you in incredible ways. When you use negative words and thoughts, the opposite is true.

The Power of Words

Throughout my life, I discovered the transformative potential of words many times! Speaking positive words and believing in myself had a ripple effect, not only on my thoughts but also on my *actions.* Most importantly, this led to successful and tangible results that improved my life in a way I could only previously *imagine.* This had an incredibly positive impact on my overall mood, my health, my work, all my relationships, including friendships, and my finances.

I was always a confident and capable person. Still, I also had many limiting ideas, was self-deprecating, and tended to see the clouds and pitfalls of every situation. There were often moments of self-doubt and feelings of "impostor syndrome"[1] despite my track record of success. I constantly sabotaged myself in both minor *and* significant ways. I always thought that seeing the possible downfalls prepared me for not encountering them. I constantly worried about everything and everyone around me, trying to control every outcome and maintain tidiness and organization. I was always aiming for perfection in every task. My goal was to present a neatly wrapped package to the world—lofty goals by any measure, considering how imperfect so much of life can be.

To say my stress levels were high is a gross understatement! I had incredibly high standards for myself and everyone around me. I was hard on everyone and secretly *so much harder* on myself. I was self-aware about my best and worst qualities and often excused how bitchy and demanding I was by saying: "At least I get things done." But, inside me, I knew the truth. After ripping someone apart, I didn't feel very good about myself. I knew that I could have handled things better. *Done* better. *Been* better.

My work ethic was all about the hustle, and I didn't yet fully understand how working smarter, not harder, could help bring balance. Don't get me wrong; I still hustle, but not with manic fervor. While sharks must keep swimming to survive, they don't always have to be at a feeding frenzy pace. My colleagues often comment on how much more mellow or "chill" I seem nowadays. The words they used in the past were nowhere near as flattering!

All the things that weighed me down, inspiring self-doubt, self-criticism, and sometimes self-loathing, are no longer part of my outlook.

Anyone can replicate the techniques and steps I used to reframe my thoughts, which is why I was encouraged to document and share my journey. A friend and a colleague, each navigating their own

---

[1] https://www.psychologytoday.com/us/basics/imposter-syndrome.

challenges and "going through it," reached out to me after noticing significant improvements in my appearance and attitude. Curious about the actions behind these transformations, they asked me to share my process. I provided them with a very quickly jotted-down list of the steps I had undertaken. Their feedback was incredibly positive; they found the steps easy to integrate into their lives and were uplifted by the results. This brought me a unique sense of joy that's hard to describe, best summed up with the old adage of: "Feeling like my cup was full." They asked if they could share my notes with friends. I said yes immediately, and they did just that. Seeing the positivity spread was very motivating. They then urged me to compile these insights into a book. And so, here we are!

Say Yes More Often!

Sometimes, the road to happiness requires embracing change and entertaining ideas that are initially uncomfortable to our logical brain. Sometimes, that logic must be put on **pause** for *a hot second*.

You may have heard that the universe has one unequivocal answer to all that we ask of it, and it is: **"YES."**

Whatever you are asking for or thinking about – the answer is always **YES**.

When you think you can do it and are happy, it says **"YES."**

If you think you are going to fail and be miserable, it says **"YES."**

The idea that "the universe always says yes" is rooted in the **Law Of Attraction**, or "LOA" for short. Some consider LOA to be one of the fundamental universal laws. Others label this concept as Pseudo-Science.

For the sake of exploration in this book, let's maintain an attitude of possibility and keep an open mind as to its *validity*. Trust me, I totally get it. You are not alone if you just groaned aloud reading the last few sentences– I also **struggled** with this one. I scolded myself over how gullible I must be even to attempt to wrap my head around this idea, let alone try to understand it. I ridiculed myself for quite some time before I decided to try and work on the presumption that it could be something worth exploring. I dismissed the concept multiple times, often laughing it off whenever it came up. It still takes some **mental gymnastics** for me to visit this idea. So don't think you're alone- if that is your opinion.

But here's the kicker: In a moment of self-reflection, I recognized that what I had been doing up until that point wasn't bringing the satisfaction I sought. Unfulfillment lingered, and things seemed to be going awry too often. A restlessness inside me didn't allow calm or peace in my life. Perhaps understanding ideas outside my comfort zone was worth looking into. After all, what did I have to lose by reading and giving it a shot?

I encourage you to adopt a similar view, allowing yourself the chance to explore all concepts. At least give it a read-through! You have my full permission to laugh and roll your eyes, too. Heaven knows I certainly did all of that and more. Feel free to breeze right past the bits that don't sit right with you. At the end of the day, I am a results-oriented person; *how I get there* is not as important to me as *making sure I reach the destination*. However, I would much prefer to **enjoy the ride**.

LOA

The LOA suggests that the energy we emit into the world – positive or negative – is what we attract back into our lives. Believing, understanding, and practicing it as if it were already true is monumental to the outcome's success.

Imagine you are a radio transmitter, and the universe is the radio receiver. When you send out signals (thoughts, emotions, beliefs, and intentions), the universe receives and responds to those signals.

Your thoughts and emotions are like *radio waves*. When you consistently focus on a particular thought, desire, or belief, it's as if you're broadcasting a radio signal.

Let's say you strongly desire to achieve a specific goal, like starting a successful business. Your thoughts and emotions regarding this goal are the signals you're sending out into the universe.

The universe, acting as the receiver, picks up on these signals. It doesn't judge or evaluate your thoughts; it simply *responds* to the energy you're projecting.

In response to your signals, the universe begins to align circumstances, people, and opportunities that match your energy.

As you continue to emit the same positive energy and maintain a strong belief in your goal, the universe's responses align more with what you want. You start to notice opportunities, resources, and synchronicities that support your journey. When you start looking for these positive changes, you see them and become more aware of these outcomes. You notice what you are looking for; the more you notice the little positive wins and gains, the happier you feel. It is a beautiful cycle that gains momentum the more you do it.

Eventually, your goal materializes in your life. You succeed in what you set out to do because the world has consistently responded with "yes" to your thoughts and desires.

The key to understanding that "the universe always says yes" is realizing that it responds to your dominant thoughts and emotions, whether positive or negative. So, keeping a positive mindset and truly focusing on what you want is incredibly important. Whatever you are thinking about – you are inviting **more** of the same!

Manifestation is the concept of calling into action and reality what we desire through the power of our thoughts, beliefs, and actions. It's about *aiming* our energy and *focusing* on our goals and dreams.

Positivity is the driving force behind manifestation. It's about maintaining a positive outlook on life, regardless of the circumstances. It's about believing in the power of possibilities, understanding that setbacks are steppingstones, and acknowledging that our thoughts *can* change our reality. It costs nothing and can change everything.

In the beginning, it can be hard to stay positive all the time, and that is why it takes practice and repetition until it becomes a habit and second nature.

So, the first step in practicing a new positive mindset is to set clear intentions. This involves identifying **what you truly desire in life**. Your intentions should be specific, positive, and achievable. For example, instead of saying, "I don't want to be stressed," you could say, "I want to experience inner peace and calm."

Second, **visualization** is a crucial aspect of realizing your desires. Once you've set clear intentions, take time each day to visualize yourself already in possession of your desires. Imagine all the little details; *feel* the happiness, emotions, and sensations associated with your goals. Visualization can help you ensure your thoughts and emotions are aligned with your desires, making the outcomes more likely to be realized.

Third, you need to use **affirmations,** which are positive statements that reinforce your intentions. Picture them as statements you make to cheer yourself on! Affirmations are *mindset boosters* that serve to reprogram your subconscious mind with empowering beliefs. Still unsure of how to do it? Try to frame the words you speak positively. Instead of saying, "I am not afraid of failure," say, "I am confident and capable of success." Likewise, **be present!** Phrase your affirmations in the present tense as if your desires are already a reality. For example, say, "I am abundant," rather than, "I will be abundant," as if the desired outcome is **already achieved**. The phrase "will be" sets it up as if it will still need to be, rather than it "already is." Setting it up as if it is always in a state of pending to happen, rather than it already having been achieved, is counterproductive. This slight distinction makes a huge difference.

Don't forget to **be specific.** Make your affirmations specific to your goals. If you want to improve your health, you could say, "I am vibrant and healthy," or "I feel good today." They don't have to be fancy statements. They just have to be clear and express what you want. Keep it simple.

Repeat your affirmations regularly, ideally daily. Consistency is key to reinforcing positive beliefs. Creating the habit takes time. I recommend giving it at least 21 days of consistent practice until it becomes almost second nature—a habit you continue to use inherently from here on out.

Shift Your Mindset, Shift Your *Reality*

The more you practice positivity, the more you can start to create a shift in your mindset, unlocking your full potential. This is applicable to all of us! In fact, it doesn't take long to realize that we are capable of achieving greatness once we set clear goals, visualize them, and work toward turning our dreams into reality. We face life's challenges with resilience and optimism, knowing they are temporary obstacles on our path to success. We learn to let go of negativity, anxiety, and self-doubt, replacing them with inner peace, confidence, and self-assurance. We start to attract positive people and opportunities into our lives, creating a **ripple effect** of joy and success.

Free will and the *freedom of choice* allow you to become a conscious co-creator of your reality. You recognize that your thoughts, feelings, and beliefs are pivotal in shaping and creating experiences. This heightened awareness allows you to take control of your life, focusing on what you want to attract rather than dwelling on what you don't want. You become more mindful of your inner dialogue and can make intentional changes to achieve your desires.

Believing you attract what you think about encourages you to take responsibility for your life. By recognizing that you have the power to shape your life, you become an active participant, not just a passive bystander. This shift boosts self-esteem and self-image, fostering confidence and resilience. Setbacks become temporary, and challenges are *reframed* as opportunities for growth.

As a bonus, as we become the best versions of ourselves, we *inspire* others to do the same. **One kindness inspires another, and so forth**; the ripple effect continues into a *cycle* of more happiness. We are ultimately creating a better, more positive world all around us.

Stop Complaining, Start Acting

Your ability to solve whatever problem you might be dealing with in your life will improve as you become more solution-oriented. Instead of dwelling on problems, you shift your focus to finding fixes and answers. You will stop complaining and start acting to solve the current task at hand. Creativity is boosted as you maneuver around any pitfalls and obstacles that arise. You will surprise yourself with **clever workarounds** when you set your mind to looking for answers instead of concentrating on the problem at hand. It is freeing to know you will always find a solution and to trust yourself and the process, as it will all turn out well in the end!

It's natural to sometimes feel whiny or complain when faced with challenges. I've found myself doing it as well. On one occasion, caught in a moment of self-pity, which wasn't common for me, I found myself venting to my little brother about the unfairness of the latest wave of challenges life had thrown my way. I lamented how it seemed like I always had to deal with more than my fair share of trials meant to "make me stronger." His response was simple yet profound: "Who better than **you** to handle life's adversities? You're a pro now. You've got this, and you'll handle it in your usual bossy, stubborn way. One way or another, you'll figure it out. You always do." He was right. I had wasted my energy on whining and complaining when I could have directed it toward tackling the issue.

To illustrate this on a relatable scale, let's consider the experience of my friend Sara. She once dreaded her daily morning commute to the city on the Long Island Rail Road. The journey was characterized by crowding, noise, delays, cancellations, and unpleasant smells, creating a miserable atmosphere. However, Sara changed her outlook and visualized smooth rides and friendly faces.

Instead of simply *complaining* about the unpleasantness, Sara decided to do something about her situation and sought alternatives. She researched, discovered a carpooling app, and joined a carpool. This completely freed up her commute and opened new opportunities to do something she *actually* liked during that time. Instead of getting annoyed at traffic and feeling like she was wasting valuable time, she used the time for learning. During the rides, she listened to great podcasts and even formed great friendships that extended beyond the ride time. She also started a women's networking club with two other carpool members. This new project not only generates income through membership dues and sponsored events but also allows her to empower other women passionately. This is something she's always wanted to do! This tiny change in her mindset sparked a series of actions and events that significantly improved Sara's overall quality of life in terms of time, finances, and fulfillment.

Think about it – could *you* be the next Sara?

This same concept is applicable to all aspects, both the big and little things in your daily life. If it can improve your quality of life, isn't it worth keeping an open mind and trying to achieve this mindset? The answer is, of course, **YES**!

In the following pages, I will include a few sample affirmations at the end of each chapter that you can use if you like. I will also include a bonus chapter of more affirmations.

Pick and choose any that resonate or *speak to you the loudest*. You can also write your own!

Keeping this in mind, here are affirmations to try out.

1. I attract what I focus on, so I focus on positivity and success.

2. My thoughts and feelings shape my reality, so I choose them wisely.

3. I attract abundance in all areas of my life.

4. My desires become my reality.

5. I am a powerful magnet for positive experiences.

6. I exude positive energy.

7. I align my thoughts and emotions with my desired outcomes.

8. I have enough of everything I want and need.

9. I am enough and feel safe at all times.

10. I trust in the process.

Chapter Two

───•◯•───

Embracing Self-Identity

I magine a world in which you simply *love yourself the way you are*. A world in which you know that despite your faults, you are still a valuable person, someone who makes other people laugh and smile, and someone who has a uniqueness to be celebrated. It's possible, and I will show you how throughout the next few pages. This chapter focuses on celebrating your unique identity, self-worth, and self-awareness. It's all about YOU!

But before we get started, let's consider what self-identity *is*. Self-identity is your unique blend of values, characteristics, and beliefs. Your life experiences and relationships shape it, all within the context of societal norms. It's your personal blueprint.

Self-worth and self-identity make quite a dynamic duo. They team up to create a positive self-image. When you genuinely believe in your worth and know yourself, confidence and positivity naturally exude from you. You **radiate it** outwards, and others can't help but respond to your positivity. It's like having a magnetic force that attracts everything you're after.

What do you need for it to work? Confidence and self-worth. Let's have a look at what these concepts entail.

Believe in Yourself!

Confidence is the first piece of the puzzle. It's that feeling you get where you feel certain of yourself and know that other people's comments won't affect your convictions.

Confidence can be built by building a solid familiarity with your identity, which is what we call *self-awareness*. Self-awareness is crucial in knowing who you are and wholeheartedly believing in yourself. It's like wearing an "I got this!" badge because you know your strengths and weaknesses and who *you* are.

When you believe in yourself, others are likely to follow suit. If you lack confidence in your abilities, it becomes challenging for others to believe in you. The key message is clear: if you don't **believe in yourself**, who will?

Know Your Worth!

Self-worth is all about recognizing and shedding self-limiting beliefs and negative self-perceptions, those pesky obstacles that keep you from turning your dreams into reality. By removing the barriers, you clear the path forward. You also make room for more things you hope for by acknowledging your worthiness and deserving nature. Challenges become speed bumps, not roadblocks, because you know your worth and keep *pushing forward*.

Imagine having a solid sense of self-worth and a clear understanding of your self-identity. When self-worth and self-identity join forces, you get inner alignment. It's like tuning all the instruments of your thoughts, emotions, beliefs, and actions to the same frequency. There is no internal resistance, just a symphony of you being your awesome self, attracting the things you desire!

Pursuing dreams becomes second nature when you believe in yourself and your abilities. When you've got a handle on these concepts, you can set specific, meaningful, and authentic goals that truly reflect who you are.

Affirm What You Want

Positive affirmations are *little love notes* to yourself. They are more effective when they are rooted in a strong sense of self-worth and self-identity. When you affirm your worthiness and align your affirmations with your authentic self, they become potent agents of bringing your thoughts to fruition.

In essence, embracing self-worth and self-identity is like laying a solid foundation. It enhances your ability to attract what you desire. It ensures harmony with your authentic self, leading to a more fulfilling and **purpose-driven life.**

1. I am a beacon of love and compassion.

2. I am resilient, strong, and brave.

3. I am constantly growing and evolving.

4. I am deserving of happiness and success.

5. I am a positive influence on the world.

6. I am confident in my unique talents and abilities.

7. I am worthy of achieving my dreams.

8. I am open to new experiences and adventures.

9. I am a creator of my own destiny.

10. I am at peace with my past and excited for my future.

Chapter Three

───●◯●───

I Believe – Cultivating Belief

Beliefs have the power to shift your reality. They can completely change whether you feel like you can do something or think it's too difficult of an obstacle to overcome. Beliefs change how you approach challenges in the same way your words put you in a positive or negative mood. In fact, the more you tell yourself something, the likelier you will be to *actually* start believing it. This chapter is about fostering beliefs that nurture your growth, affirm your potential, and enhance your overall happiness.

Believe You *Can* Get Past That Hurdle

If you believe in your limitations or the impossibility of your desires coming true, you're likely to end up with **only** those limitations and obstacles. Cultivating belief helps you align your thoughts and expectations with what you want to achieve, once again increasing the likelihood of it becoming a reality.

Many people harbor limiting beliefs that stem from past experiences, societal conditioning, or self-doubt. These beliefs can act as barriers to success and happiness. These doubts set up **mental blockades** to your momentum and progress. By actively cultivating positive and empowering thoughts, you can *overcome* these limitations. Positivity creates a more supportive mental environment for fulfilling your desires. Take the time to work on your beliefs about yourself. You will never regret the time you spent caring for yourself and finding happiness.

Belief in oneself and one's ability to achieve outcomes is closely tied to self-confidence. When you believe in your capacity to attract what you desire, you naturally become more confident in your actions. This increased self-assuredness can help you take the necessary steps to achieve your goals. Everyone around you will notice a difference, and you will feel a change in how they treat you.

On the other hand, you will find that no one else's opinion **matters as much** anymore when you carry yourself with self-confidence. You set the tone for how others view and treat you by knowing who you are and understanding that you are worthy of their respect, time, and love. When I was worried about how I looked and what I wore in social settings, my brother-in-law often reminded me: "It doesn't matter what you are wearing, as long as you wear it with confidence." He was always right. The minute I would straighten my spine, push back my shoulders, hold my head just a bit higher, or flash a huge smile- no one looked past the determined look in my eyes long enough to worry or care about what outfit I had put together. Not only that, I also cared a *whole lot less* about what they were thinking as I took a stance of confidence.

Understand That Your Beliefs Are Powerful!

Belief acts as a magnetic force that aligns your energy with your desires. When you truly believe in something, you emit a strong and consistent energy that resonates with what you want to attract.

When you believe something is possible, you are more likely to *pursue and attain* it. If you think you can win the prize you desire, you try harder and make more moves to your advantage. The opposite is also true; if you think you *can't* accomplish something, you will probably not work as hard for the desired outcome. The reason you won't work as hard is that your subconscious *already* thinks it will be a waste of time since you aren't going to get what you want anyway. You must **flip the belief switch to the "ON" position** inside your mind to get what you want. The goal is to convince your subconscious of the **plausibility** of an attainable result.

Believe That You *Can* Do It

Developing a mindset of persistence and resilience is crucial in cultivating belief. Although you may encounter challenges or setbacks along your journey, solid belief in your goals can help you remain committed and resilient in the face of adversity. It is important to persevere even during difficult moments, knowing that everything will work out in the end. You will undoubtedly find the solutions to solve your problems as you clear your mind of doubt and allow yourself the time to put things in perspective.

Belief is *not* just a mental concept; it's deeply tied to your emotions. When you genuinely believe in something, you feel a sense of emotional connection and passion. This emotional charge adds power to your intentions, actions, and steps toward achieving your ultimate goals.

You are enough, and as such, you can achieve anything you set your mind to. If you can *envision it*, you can *do whatever it takes* to make it a reality. By believing in yourself and your abilities and keeping a mindset of persistence, tenacity, and resilience, you can overcome pretty much anything life throws at you.

By nurturing positive and empowering beliefs, you create a fertile ground for your desires to blossom and bear fruit.

Positivity will help bolster your confidence and help you stay resilient on your self-improvement or growth journey. It's an essential step in the **deliberate creation** of the life you want to live.

Belief may be the *hardest thing we ever do* as it often requires faith in things we *cannot touch or see.*

1. I believe in my endless potential.

2. I believe every challenge is a steppingstone to success.

3. I believe in the beauty of my dreams.

4. I believe in love as the greatest force.

5. I believe in my power to create change.

6. I believe in new beginnings.

7. I believe in finding good in every situation.

8. I believe in the strength of my spirit.

9. I believe in the journey as much as the destination.

10. I believe in the light that I bring to the world.

Chapter Four

I Feel– Connecting with Emotions

We all have emotions. We *all* feel things, some of us more than others. Unfortunately, we live in a day and age where we see *rationality* as something to always look up to and *emotions* as things to avoid at all costs. And yet, this is unnecessary – why can't we accept that, as human beings, we have emotions and that they are *part of who we are*? In this chapter, we do just this. Here, you are asked to deeply **connect** with your emotions, understanding their importance in shaping your overall well being.

"I Feel" Statements

One technique to start out with is using "I Feel" statements. This tool can not only help you identify the root of your emotions but also allow you to respond to them with positivity and clarity.

Emotions are powerful signals that reflect your inner state. When you start to use "I Feel" statements, you acknowledge and express your emotional state, which is a key component of the frequency you emit to the world and others.

Let's take a look at a few examples of "I Feel" statements:

- "I feel grateful for the support of my friends and family."
- "I feel anxious about my meeting."
- "I feel excited to start this new project."
- "I feel sad about not getting the promotion."

Your emotions are crucial in indicating how aligned you are with your desires. If you are experiencing positive emotions like gratitude, joy, and enthusiasm, it means that you are in *alignment* with what you want. Conversely, negative emotions such as doubt, fear, and frustration signal *a lack* of alignment. By using "I Feel" statements to acknowledge your emotions, you can become more aware of whether you need to make adjustments. It's like a thermostat reading of just how "hot" or "cold" you are in terms of being in the *sweet spot* for everything to be comfortable and for all to fall into place as it should. So, adjust the dial as needed.

Acknowledging your emotions through "I Feel" statements is an empowering practice. It encourages self-awareness and *self-expression*, which are essential for personal growth and transformation. When you take ownership of your emotions, you are better equipped to make intentional choices. Using these statements to express your positive emotions *amplifies* those feelings. When you articulate positive emotions, you enhance your ability to attract experiences and circumstances that match those emotions.

Our emotions serve as an **internal guidance system**. You are tuning into this system when you express how you feel. "I Feel" statements can also express and *release* negative emotions or resistance that may be blocking your success. By acknowledging and articulating these feelings, you can process and *let go* of them, clearing the path for more positive results. Basically, they help you **get out of your own way**!

Not only this, but emotions add depth and clarity to your intentions. You provide a clear and focused signal by saying, "I Feel," followed by a positive sentiment related to your desire. This specificity helps everyone around you respond more precisely to your requests.

When you visualize your desires, try to incorporate the "I Feel" aspect by imagining how you would feel when your wishes come true. This will intensify the emotional experience and make your visualizations more vivid.

Connect with Your Emotions

Now, let's delve into the life-changing impact of connecting with your emotions. Emotions are potent and can significantly impact experiences. Whether it's immense joy or deep sadness, the intensity of emotions can add depth and complexity to any circumstance. For instance, consider emotions in moments like reuniting with a loved one at the airport or attending a funeral for someone you care about deeply. In both these polar opposite situations, the intensity of emotions can bring tears to your eyes, showcasing how complex feelings can be. Tears of sadness, tears of happiness. We have different emotions leading to each part of this spectrum. We can work through the emotions as long as we deal with them and not deny them. That is why connecting with what we feel is imperative.

For example, as a working mother, I dealt with *all kinds of emotions*. I was on planes and traveled away from home often, sometimes several days a month. I also had *tremendous* anxiety about preparing everything in advance for all possible scenarios – kids' assignments, meals for the week, activities, rides, instructions for their caretaker in my absence, medical care authorizations, and the list goes on. Despite all the preparation, time, and effort I took to ensure the impact of my being gone was limited, the pressure was daunting. I still felt **guilt** and **stress** that I hadn't done enough. The worry continued on my trips, and my concern for my children's well-being and safety played in the back of my head every day as background noise in my brain. It did terrible things to my concentration and robbed me of sleep. I wasn't connected to my emotions. Instead, I was trying to cope with them by being in control of everything else. I felt like I was constantly running behind a wheel that was rolling in a field, the wheel that was my life, trying not to let it get too far ahead of me, or I wouldn't be able to **catch it** before it *fell off the cliff*. After constantly feeling drained and lacking work-life balance, I began using "I Feel" statements to articulate my emotions. Instead of staying silent about my overwhelm, I admitted I felt stressed and needed to do something about it. This new clarity was like a release valve. It led me to assess what I needed to really do, really worry about, and shift priorities. All of these changes led to an improved sense of well-being. A deeper sense of calm ensued. More importantly, I have a more fulfilled life, personally and professionally.

There were other times I felt similarly overwhelmed with responsibility. After my husband passed away, I had to juggle work and fill the role of being both mom and dad. The financial burden and responsibility also fell on my shoulders. I was either a good mom or a great businesswoman during this time, but something was always falling off on one side of the scale for the other to be great. Frankly, I felt that my children deserved more. I was always so busy at work, and even at home, I was multi-tasking responsibilities. Like most parents, I was managing a household, planning, cooking, cleaning, paying bills, doing laundry, filling the fridge, chauffeuring children to events, and juggling the 100 other things involved in raising a family. I finally admitted, "I feel less than and want more quality time with my kids. They deserve better." This acknowledgment prompted me to re-evaluate everything. I rescheduled my day to ensure that what mattered most was being taken care of and that things that weren't as urgent were assigned to others. It is important to note that most of the responsibilities I was bending under the weight of were responsibilities no one asked me to take on; I just always wanted to do as much as possible. If I wasn't juggling a hundred balls in the air simultaneously, I wasn't happy, but it was **also** the cause of my **misery**. Letting go of some control was amazingly freeing. This set of moves allowed me to carve out dedicated time for what was really important. The result was a more harmonious family life and **a lot less guilt.**

Another example is when I sensed a growing distance and lack of connection in one of my oldest friendships. I realized I was partly to blame as life gets busy, and sometimes, the day-to-day responsibilities get in the way. Reflecting on these feelings, I admitted, "I feel disconnected and miss the closeness we used to have." This honest expression prompted me to reach out and initiate a heartfelt conversation, strengthen communication, and invest more time in nurturing that relationship. The result was a more profound sense of connection and a more fulfilling social life. It filled a huge void. Even though I am lucky to have unique, long-lasting friendships with so many of my friends, both near and far, around the globe- this bond was one I am glad I took the time to rekindle. Certain friendships are so deep that you can pick up where you left off, finishing each other's sentences and thoughts. The kind where you always end up laughing so hard your sides hurt. If I hadn't acknowledged it or shifted the responsibility to them alone, we may have drifted and missed out on the happiness reconnecting has brought to our lives.

Utilizing "I Feel" statements and connecting with your emotions is integral to cultivating a positive mindset. This practice empowers you to make intentional choices, signaling the outcomes you wish to achieve. By embracing your feelings in this manner, you not only enhance your emotional intelligence but also elevate the effectiveness of your ability to usher in transformative changes in your life!

1. I feel gratitude for every blessing in my life.

2. I feel joy in every moment, big or small.

3. I feel love deeply and unconditionally.

4. I feel connected to the peace within me.

5. I feel the strength of my emotions.

6. I feel calm in the face of challenges.

7. I feel the beauty of life in every breath I take.

8. I feel my heart open to endless possibilities.

9. I feel the warmth of kindness surrounding me.

10. I feel my feelings without judgment or fear.

Chapter Five

—————•◉•—————

I Speak – The Power of Words

Words have the incredible power to shape our lives and the world around us. They allow us to speak to ourselves and others, sharing a message that may have a greater impact than we may think. In this chapter, we'll explore how you can harness this power to create positive change and empower yourself.

How do Words Impact Your Thoughts?

The words you use have legitimate sway in your thoughts. When you *consciously* choose positive and empowering words, you are more likely to have positive and empowering thoughts. This foundational alignment between your language and desires kick-starts *change*.

As we have seen, spoken and repeated affirmations act as quick, little confidence-saving **antidotes for the poisons we feed ourselves** in the forms of *negative thoughts* or *self-deprecating talk*.

But we haven't yet explored *why* affirmations work. Well, positive affirmations are believed to work by **rewiring the neural pathways in the brain, allowing individuals to change their thought patterns and beliefs.** This is called **neuroplasticity**[2]. Repetition of affirmations essentially helps fortify neural connections. By repeating positive affirmations out loud regularly, you *reinforce* your ideas and expectations, paving the way for a more optimistic and productive mindset.

———————————

[2] **https://www.ncbi.nlm.nih.gov/books/NBK557811/#:~:text=It%20is%20defined%20as%20the ,traumatic%20brain%20injury%20(TBI).**

That being said, **the language you use can mold your beliefs about yourself, your abilities, and how you see the world around you.** When you speak in ways that support your goals and aspirations, you cultivate beliefs that align with what you want to achieve.

When you speak well of others and lift them up, as we should do whenever possible, you also set *them* up for **success**. They will rise and bloom to the kind words and strive harder to live up to the expectations set by your comments. But of course, the opposite is also true.

Take a moment to ask yourself – do you feel like you mainly speak in a positive manner or a *negative* one? In the past, my "go-to mode" was to be sarcastic and ironic and focus on the gloom or doom. The downside often dominated my speech patterns, even when setting up a joke or quip. When we become aware of the way we tend to speak, we can make changes and improvements. So, it is worth taking a second to self-evaluate.

Verbalizing your intentions clarifies your goals and acts as a **catalyst for action.** Your words serve as a clear signal to both you and the world about your aspirations. They become the motivation for the steps needed to translate goals into reality. When you articulate your goals and aspirations, you create a clear and specific **focus** for your efforts to be *aimed toward*. When you voice your desires and feelings, you are erasing the possibility of doubts or misunderstandings. There is *crystal* clarity in speaking things out loud. You can catch and correct yourself as you say it; if it doesn't sound authentic or it is **not** really what you want – you **will** hear it!

Words have the transformative potential to become **self-fulfilling prophecies**. Upbeat and confident speech patterns increase the likelihood of taking actions essential for goal achievement. These goals don't just appear achieved; you take steps and actions to achieve the desired results. But it starts with speaking the thought out loud. First, to yourself and then to others as you begin to take the steps needed to get to where you want to be.

Consider my friend Lisa, who battled self-doubt in her career. Through daily affirmations such as "I am capable and deserving of success," she gradually transformed her mindset, bolstering her confidence. Within a year, she achieved the promotion she didn't previously think she could get! By using affirmations, she spoke her intentions and, with practice over time, started believing what she was telling herself. She basically used a **"fake it till you make it"** mantra in her process. Her manager reviewed her performance, telling her: "I have watched you get more confident and ask for the tools you needed to complete projects earlier than the deadline, and your work quality is better than ever." She was very proud as she shared this story with me!

Blake, another friend, also practiced affirmations to lead a healthier lifestyle. He had a terrible complex of being scrawny and not having muscle definition. He always felt lanky in his clothes, and this caused him to hunch over when he walked. By articulating his goals of doing regular strength training exercises and eating increased protein-based calories, he clarified his desires and eliminated doubts. This laid the groundwork for tangible progress. Each day, he added *another* task to his affirmation and action list, and the list grew, and the tasks were accomplished. Nine months later, he had changed how his body looked and how he looked at himself. Others noticed as well! He often tells me how much more confident he feels shopping for clothes and going on dates. Maybe you also relate to this – as we all have some things we are self-conscious about!

Maybe you are someone who has spoken positively to others about bettering yourself and reaching your goals. This verbal commitment you shared with others likely held you accountable and motivated you to follow through with your goals– something you may have put off without telling people about it! Maybe you *knew* you had to do it since you had *already* told people. Accountability is a powerful motivator.

Remember, the words you use have the power to mold your reality, so **choose them carefully** and **use them intentionally.**

Deliberate and mindful use of language is the golden key! With continuous practice, you can witness firsthand how the power of your words can add *dimension* to your life. So, try affirming your aspirations daily. This might lead you to take small but consistent and concrete steps that have a *huge* impact.

1. I speak about my truth with courage.

2. I speak words that heal, not harm.

3. I speak with love, kindness, and empathy.

4. I speak blessings into my life every day.

5. I speak with authenticity and integrity.

6. I speak to myself with the same kindness I offer others.

7. I speak positively about my future.

8. I speak affirmations that empower me.

9. I speak with the wisdom of a thoughtful mind.

10. I speak to inspire and uplift those around me.

Chapter Six

────•◦○◦•────

I Hear – Listening

H ave you ever met someone with whom having a discussion felt *absolutely draining?* You may have tried many times to be their friend, to talk to and *listen* to them, but the favor was never returned. After a while, you may have realized that this friendship was entirely one-sided, and you stopped making an effort to meet them. Welcome to Chapter Six, where we delve into the significance of *active listening* and its potential impact on your personal and professional life. Throughout this chapter, you'll find techniques to enhance your listening skills and learn how to apply them in your day-to-day interactions.

Listening Is Just as Important as Speaking

Listening is as crucial as speaking, urging you to attune to the messages emanating from your surroundings and inner self. It will help you embrace the wisdom of the world around you. There is great skill in knowing when to speak and when to listen instead.

Authentic listening, which is a special kind of listening, involves paying attention to your inner guidance, intuition, and gut feelings. Aligning with your inner self will help you make choices and decisions that are in harmony with your desires and goals, allowing for actions congruent with your intentions. This is why it's crucial to listen instead of speaking. Sometimes, you must *hear* yourself instead of drowning out the noise with your thoughts.

In other words, to effectively realize your goals and desires, you must clearly and precisely understand what they are. Listening to your **inner voice** clarifies your true desires and well-defined intentions and garners more responsive outcomes from everyone and everything around you. Knowing what you want is the primary step in getting it.

Likewise, listening to your **intuition** helps you to make informed decisions, increasing the likelihood of successful outcomes. This advantage stems from choosing actions and paths that resonate with your goals.

Becoming an attentive listener equips you to identify opportunities and take *inspired actions* efficiently. This skill **accelerates** the achievement of your desires. This tool fosters awareness of options, benefits, and opportunities often overlooked in negative thinking and self-doubt. Take the time to listen and notice!

You Can Benefit From Listening More

Let me tell you a story that might show you what I mean more specifically. Years ago, early in my career, my brilliant employer emphasized the importance of listening to and understanding the client's perspective, stating, "M, I know you're smart. You don't have to keep proving that to me or the clients. I already know what WE know. I want to know what THEY are thinking and what THEY know. That is what gives us an advantage in meeting their needs." I had been *so* focused on being impressive and proving how prepared and informed I was and what I could bring to the table that I talked too much and didn't listen enough. I missed the opportunity to *fully* give the clients what they really wanted and expected. Sometimes, listening involves setting aside **ego**!

Listening for Inspiration

Listening is also about tuning into positive and uplifting messages from your surroundings, creating a positive mindset. The principle is simple: **if you listen, you will learn more.**

Listening actively reinforces your faith when you observe synchronicities or positive results – it *inspires you*. When you hear evidence of someone else's success, it becomes easier for you to believe that you can achieve the same outcome or replicate the success. This increased faith enhances your ability to achieve your desires, creating a cycle that begins with active listening.

In fact, by listening patiently to *yourself*, your intuition, and the *little voice* inside you, you align yourself with divine timing, trusting that everything will fall into place when it's meant to.

Listening involves being grateful for the messages and signs received. Gratitude amplifies positive energy, attracting more of what you're thankful for into your life. Acknowledge and celebrate the little wins until the big ones unfold. Listening allows you to open yourself to wisdom, guidance, and support.

Below are some listening techniques you can use:

1. Reflective Listening:

Method: Repeat what you've heard in your own words.

Practice: After a conversation, summarize the key points to ensure understanding and show genuine interest in others.

2. Empathetic Listening:

Method: Put yourself in the speaker's shoes to try and understand their emotions.

Practice: Acknowledge and validate others' feelings without judgment, fostering a supportive environment.

3. Mindful Listening:

Method: Focus entirely on the speaker without distractions.

Practice: Turn off electronic devices, maintain eye contact, and actively engage in conversation to enhance understanding.

4. Appreciative Listening:

Method: Seek out and appreciate the positive aspects of what others are saying.

Practice: Acknowledge and highlight the strengths and positive contributions of the speaker to cultivate optimism.

5. Solution-Focused Listening:

Method: Focus on finding solutions rather than dwelling on problems.

Practice: Encourage conversations to steer towards actionable steps and resolutions, promoting a problem-solving mindset.

Listening is a simple and graceful way to show respect, understanding, and care. It allows us to **reciprocate** and connect with our loved ones, mentors, colleagues and the world around us.

Only by listening can we **truly hear** what we need to know, enabling us to connect with others **in a way that speaking cannot.**

1. I hear the world guiding me with love.

2. I hear the truth in my heart.

3. I hear the call of my soul's deepest desires.

4. I hear wisdom in silence.

5. I hear whispers of hope in moments of doubt.

6. I hear joy in the laughter of others.

7. I hear the rhythm of life in every heartbeat.

8. I hear the answers I seek in quiet moments.

9. I hear the harmony of nature's song.

10. I hear love in every kind word spoken to me.

Chapter Seven

I Write – The Power of the Pen

As human beings, we communicate in *many ways*. We speak to people, we listen to them, and we even position our bodies in a certain way to send a certain message. But there's another way we communicate: by *writing*. So, let's dive into the power a pen can wield.

Writing as a Tool

Writing serves as a potent tool for achieving your dreams and goals. It inspires you to express your thoughts and desires, transforming them from abstract concepts to tangible realities. Writing compels you to crystallize your intentions, offering a clear and detailed representation of what you wish to create. Clarity is crucial, as specific, well-defined intentions readily garner responses. If you aim to achieve your goals, consider putting them down on paper!

That being said, writing requires you to focus your energy and attention on your *desires*. As you repeatedly write affirmations, goals, or intentions, you concentrate your thoughts and emotions on what you want to achieve.

Writing lets you draw out your desires as if they have already materialized. This technique sends a potent message about your intentions. Your written words create a mental image, allowing you to feel and experience your desires vividly. You paint the canvas with words until the image is clear and *mirrors* your aspirations. The more you write things down, the more they become *concrete* in your mind. In other words, it works as another way to *convince* yourself.

Reprogram Your Mind

Reprogramming your subconscious mind is possible by writing positive statements reinforcing your beliefs and desires. These statements help replace *limiting beliefs* with empowering ones, aligning your mindset with your wishes.

Repetition is vital to embedding these thoughts and emotions into your subconscious, making them a natural part of your belief system. And you guessed it – the more you write, the more you fortify your beliefs and abilities.

In fact, writing can be a therapeutic tool for releasing negative emotions, doubts, and fears that may block your thought process and ability to act. When you write about your concerns or challenges, you acknowledge and release them. This creates space for positive energy and a constructive way forward. It is effectively a way to find an escape hatch for the negative thoughts and feelings you might have that could be holding you back from living the life you really want to live!

Jotting down your goals and intentions proves to be a potent tool for achieving success. This simple act instills a sense of commitment and accountability, motivating you to take action. It also helps you stay focused!

Writing allows you to **track your progress and celebrate your achievements.** Documenting the outcomes that have already occurred reinforces your belief in your ability to succeed. This practice becomes particularly valuable when faced with challenges or setbacks. By looking back at how far you have come, you can find the motivation to keep moving forward!

Ultimately, writing can help you *rewire* your mind. You may wonder: how can it **possibly** do this? Well, writing by hand stimulates the cells in the part of the brain called the **RAS**[3], or the Reticular

---

[3] https://www.hurleywrite.com/blog/The-Impact-of-Writing-on-the-Brain-Revealed#:~:text=The%20act%20of%20writing%20itself,on%20processing%20what%20you%20write.

Activating System. RAS acts as a filter and decides what to *focus* on immediately. It filters other things *out*. Writing activates your RAS to engrain knowledge into your memory. Bypassing your critical mind, writing communicates directly with the part of your mind that influences your beliefs and behaviors. This is a nifty little shortcut to realign your thoughts and actions with your goals and aspirations.

Keep a Journal

Keeping a journal is a practical and tangible way to record your thoughts, experiences, and achievements. Whether it's your wishes, goals, or any synchronicities you notice, writing them down can help you gain clarity and insight into your life.

The recommended frequency is at least once a day, but ultimately, it's up to you and what feels most comfortable. Whether every morning, night, or once a week, stick to what **works best for you**!

Journaling can be fun, I promise! In attempting to conquer my daily morning workouts. I started a quirky workout journal, chronicling hilarious mishaps to stay motivated. For example, a pose that seemed to blur the line between Zen and sneezing. Picture this: a sudden sneeze struck mid-sun salutation, transforming a serene yoga pose into a spontaneous interpretative *"Achoo"* dance. The journal entry was titled "Sneezasana." You had to be there to fully appreciate the funny part! The journal became a comic relief and a written testament to my resilience in the face of accidental gymnastics. I can't stop laughing when I look back at what happened when I attempted modified jumping jacks, forgetting I still had on my resistance bands. It gave new meaning to *defying gravity* as I tried to extricate myself from the tangled bands. I can tell you that it became evident that **my best workout companion was a sense of humor.**

Let your words craft a story that's as extraordinary as you are! Enjoy the outlet a pen and paper can offer. Keep writing, keep laughing, and watch amazing changes unfold as you progress towards your goals!

1. I write my aspirations with conviction and faith.

2. I write my thoughts with clarity and purpose.

3. I write my story with courage and authenticity.

4. I write down my achievements and celebrate them.

5. I write to express my deepest emotions.

6. I write affirmations that resonate with my soul.

7. I write to connect with my inner wisdom.

8. I write to release what no longer serves me.

9. I write to create a life of joy and fulfillment.

10. I write gratitude lists to remind me of my blessings.

Chapter Eight

————•◦◯◦•————

Wealth and Abundance Mindset

Wealth is more than financial gain; it's about *creating abundance* in **all** life areas. Life is also about more than just creating financial wealth. It's about living in a way that makes you feel **fulfilled** in *all* areas. This chapter is dedicated to fostering a mindset that attracts prosperity in all its possibilities. Abundance includes financial success and having **more than enough** of everything you want and need.

Your Mindset for Abundance

Fostering a mindset that attracts prosperity is a process that involves changing your beliefs, thoughts, and behaviors. These techniques can help you cultivate a mindset of abundance and attract financial success into your life.

Start by recognizing any limiting beliefs you may have about money and success. A limiting belief is simply a belief that holds you back from working on yourself or believing something *better* about yourself. These could include beliefs like "Money is scarce," "I'm not good with money," "I don't deserve wealth," or "I don't have enough."

Then, **challenge these limiting beliefs** by examining their **validity.** Remove the idea of not having enough or scarcity from your thinking and language. Replace them with empowering beliefs such as "Money flows to me easily and constantly from multiple sources," "I am capable of managing my finances wisely," and "I deserve financial abundance."

In other words, you need to *believe* in your ability to succeed. You need to believe that you **can** be great and that all your dreams and goals *are* achievable! Trust me, it's not an easy process, but it's *so* worth it in the end!

Achieving Financial Success

To achieve financial success, there are several habits you can cultivate. These habits are there to keep you *on track* with your goals. But first, you need to develop a habit of **gratitude** by acknowledging and appreciating the abundance you already have in your life. Focus on the present moment and express gratitude for your health, relationships, and the resources available to you. Actively look for things you are thankful for and appreciate the little gains. The more we see the things we already have to be grateful for, the more we realize that we can *add* to them instead of feeling like we have to start from nothing!

Next, create a habit of vision. Form a clear and **vivid mental image** of your success. Imagine yourself achieving your financial goals, whether it's buying a house, starting a business, or becoming debt-free. Visualize the details, emotions, and experiences associated with your success. This will help you stay motivated and focused. Take a moment right now to do that. Picture whatever it is you want.

Make sure that you **define clear and achievable financial goals**. Break them down into smaller, actionable steps. Doing so helps your brain accept that these micro goals are attainable. Setting goals gives you direction and a sense of purpose, which is crucial for achieving financial success. These goals help you feel like they are achievable, motivating you to work on them!

Using positive affirmations related to financial success can also be helpful. Repeat these affirmations daily to reinforce your belief in your ability to gain prosperity. Examples include "I am financially abundant," "I attract wealth effortlessly," and "Money flows to me from various sources."

Finally, **invest in your personal and financial education.** Continuously expand your knowledge about money management, investments, and financial planning. The more you know, the more confident you'll feel about handling your finances. But for that, you need to view yourself as a continuous learner! What separates the most successful people from those who aren't is that successful people constantly learn and look for ways to improve themselves. They always stay on top by not getting complacent. We could *all* benefit from learning more, so make some time for learning every day! Implementing these habits can help you succeed and live the life you want.

Get Educated

As mentioned above, knowledge is key. So, take the time to research different types of accounts that earn money with the money you put into them passively. If you want to improve your financial situation, developing multiple revenue streams is essential, no matter how small the amounts are. The key is to get into the habit of having money constantly flowing in from different sources and allowing it to grow over time.

Investing in well-researched and dependable investment opportunities, even in small amounts, is smart. This can be any amount and it doesn't have to be complicated or fancy!

Take advantage of your banks' and credit cards' free financial services.

Choose products and financial avenues that you feel comfortable using. This can be as simple as opening a high-yield savings account or investing in certificates of deposit (CDs). Other options include investing in dividend stocks or bonds with a broker or app. If your company has a retirement plan and matching program, you can up your contribution. Whatever you choose, ensure you take time to vet and study before making any decisions. **Always research** before entrusting someone with your money and **be vigilant against scams.**

If finance scares or intimidates you and you are looking for smaller-scale income boosts, that is also relatively easy enough to do. If you have time available, consider a **side hustle** you can do that relates to something you are passionate about or enjoy doing. Do you like baking? Bake on the weekends and sell baked goods to family, friends, and coworkers or at local markets. Do you like correcting people? Then edit their blogs or write on freelance websites. Do you like photography or painting? Set up exhibits at your libraries or community events. Are you saving the bees by beekeeping and planting flowers? Sell your honey at the local farmer's market. There are even positions available online for empathetic listeners. Annotate, edit, illustrate, layout, or record audio. There are many opportunities to explore income-generating positions that allow you to decide how much of your available time and effort you want to dedicate. Whether you have one to two hours each evening or a whole day on the weekend, it is up to you to decide.

These days, you can set up a YouTube channel, review products you have already purchased, write a blog, rent out useful tools, or even rent out your home when you are away. Empty your closets and house of items and clothes you no longer use. You can resell them at a garage sale or through many online sites. This gives you the double whammy of freeing up closet and shelf space, decluttering, and making extra cash. It doesn't always require monetary investment to be able to generate a little additional flow of income. Sometimes, it just takes your time and effort. No matter what your financial goals are, try to frame them as daily or monthly objectives. For instance, $300 a month is $10 a day. While aiming for an extra $3,000 a month means striving for $100 a day in additional income. Whatever your financial needs or goals are, you can define them in terms your brain will allow you to believe it is possible to achieve. There are practical, manageable, and **believable** actions you can take immediately to solve financial situations. The important part is to get busy doing something.

Be Smart with Your Financial Goals

Success can seem unattainable. It's sometimes difficult to see success as something that's achievable because, to many of us, it feels like something we see *other* people reach. But that's where we are wrong. We have to see the world for what it has to offer us! We have to do the work and convince ourselves that we, too, can reach that point!

Taking deliberate and inspired actions toward your goals is essential to achieving financial success. This involves more than just hoping for a miracle or wishing for things to happen. Instead, you must **align your thoughts and intentions** with practical steps to help you reach your objectives. Be on the lookout for opportunities, save money, invest wisely, and *always* move forward toward your goals.

It would be best to surround yourself with positive and supportive people who believe in your financial success. Don't let anyone talk you out of your ideas or bring your spirits down. Avoid individuals who are negative or discourage your aspirations. These people are like energy "vampires." Not in the literal sense, but figuratively speaking! They seem to suck the joy right out of you and can leave you feeling drained or mentally and emotionally exhausted after an encounter. Limit the time spent with these types of characters to little or none! If the people surrounding you aren't your biggest cheerleaders, you need a new team. Period.

Now, this next one is hard for some people. Don't fear money or making it. Fear is the most significant barrier to success. You might not even know you fear it, but many do because it's the *unknown*. And yet, it's something we can *learn*. You can be smart about educating yourself and learn at your own pace.

Remember that patience is key to wealth creation and success. Trust the process and believe that your desires are on their way. There is a downright ridiculous amount of wealth in this world. You deserve to have wealth just as much as anyone else.

Be Generous

It's essential to practice generosity by giving back to others. Sharing what you have creates a positive flow of energy and abundance. Nothing compares to the feeling of giving to others, of being generous, and of having enough to share. It is one of the most fulfilling and satisfying feelings of our lifetime. Why? Because we feel like we are **living our purpose**. We aren't keeping it all to ourselves – we're helping other people reach *their* goals.

My parents embodied incredible generosity. My dad, the radiant smile of our family, had a heart even bigger than his infectious smile, sharing everything with anyone. Equally remarkable was my mother, the most giving person I've ever known.

It wasn't until later in life that I grasped the rarity of her level of generosity. Growing up, she selflessly gave to her children, neighbors, church, extended family, friends, and even strangers. I vividly recall her taking off her shoes and handing them over to someone who needed them more. Stories abound of her leaping out of a moving car or sprinting across a busy highway to aid those in need. These weren't isolated incidents but rather a recurring theme that transformed her into a local legend.

Our home often hosted strangers she befriended, providing them with a meal and money, clothes, and essentials gathered from around the house. Witnessing her compassion taught us the importance of giving not just possessions but a piece of ourselves. Even now, I strive to emulate her, giving until it hurts.

Miraculously, there was always enough. Her unyielding faith in a positive outcome for our family continues to inspire me. Her appreciation of the beauty of life and the unwavering belief that everything would be alright shaped my values. Her ability to forgive others and still be kind to them after they had wronged her was also incredible to me. I have *shamefully* made that poor woman cry on more than one occasion, and not once did that let it stop her from always being there no matter what I needed. She still looks at me like I am a gift to unwrap when I walk into a room. She lights up like a kid on Christmas morning, instantly making me **feel safe and loved**. There is an unconditional love inside her that exudes in all she does, and I have yet to see it replicated quite the same in anyone or anywhere else. Even more so than what we would often describe as a "Mother's love." This forgiveness *she personifies* is also a form of giving and generosity.

To this day, I find comfort in the idea that giving, whether in time or resources, is a profound gift to one's spirit and soul. Moreover, as I continue to draw inspiration from my mother's selfless acts, it's worth noting that fostering a giving spirit can extend to various aspects of life. It will bring you joy when you can share what you have, knowing confidently that you will always **have enough to share**.

Be Ready to Face Challenges

On a completely different note, a helpful tip is to keep a money journal or spreadsheet to track your financial progress. It will be fun to celebrate your achievements, no matter how small. It has the added benefit of helping you keep track of your growing finances and any challenges that arise.

Challenges are likely to arise on your financial journey. But, instead of dwelling on any setbacks, focus on solutions and stay positive. Use challenges as opportunities for growth and learning. Sometimes, you must take a step backward before leaping forward.

Be open to unexpected opportunities and sources of income. Opportunities and abundance are often delivered in unexpected ways. Stay open-minded to new ideas.

We all have stories about missed opportunities. I wish I had listened to my taxi driver in Vegas many years ago, who told me I should invest in something called "Bitcoin." That was the literal TIP the fare he had driven right before me had given him. When he explained it was digital currency, I burst out laughing at him and declined, still giggling at the absurdity when I exited the cab. Little did I know what that "absurdity" would become in the years that followed. Well, we all know how that story went and how much of a fool I was not to look into this advice. A huge, missed opportunity! One of the dumbest choices ever! But it makes a funny story to tell, and we have to be able to laugh at ourselves.

Review your financial goals regularly to stay aligned with your desires. Adjust your goals as needed to reflect your evolving aspirations. Be actively engaged in making changes as needed.

Finally, remember that attracting financial success is not only about thinking positively; it's about aligning your thoughts, beliefs, and actions with your financial goals. You can create your desired financial success with dedication, persistence, and a mindset of abundance. Before you know it, the gains will add up, and you will have all you need and more.

1. I have enough of all I need.

2. Wealth flows to me effortlessly.

3. I make wise investment choices.

4. My wealth is growing exponentially.

5. I deserve a prosperous and financially stable life.

6. I attract lucrative opportunities that increase my wealth.

7. My actions create a constant flow of prosperity.

8. I am surrounded by abundance in all areas of my life.

9. I use my wealth to positively impact the world.

10. Every decision I make leads to greater abundance and fulfillment.

Chapter Nine

————————•◯•————————

Cultivating Self-Love

S elf-love is essential for a fulfilling life. When you love and value yourself, you emit an energy that aligns you with positive experiences, people, and opportunities. Conversely, self-doubt and self-criticism can cause you to project or emit an unsure and depressed energy that can attract negativity and limitations. It will start to repel people, partners, and opportunities. This chapter is about helping you *love yourself* just as you are.

When In Doubt, Focus on Your Worth

Self-doubt and self-criticism are common obstacles preventing you from embracing your self-worth and self-identity. They can present in various ways, such as negative self-talk, comparing yourself to others, and excessive self-blame. Please don't believe the lies we sometimes whisper to ourselves to self-sabotage our progress. You may feel anxious, insecure, or overwhelmed when you doubt your abilities or worth. Sometimes, you may avoid taking risks or pursuing your goals altogether due to fear of failure or rejection.

Thankfully, there are solutions for this! Indeed, practicing self-love can help you overcome fear and self-doubt. This means you will have greater courage to step out of your comfort zone, take risks, and pursue your dreams without fear. You will feel empowered to take charge of your life and make choices that align with your values and desires. You will also be much less likely to be influenced by external opinions or societal expectations! Imagine just that – a world in which you are convinced that whatever you are doing is right *for you* and not letting others affect your confidence. It might sound impossible, but if I could do it, so can you!

Unfortunately, many of us **fail to see our worth** and forget to love ourselves because it's much easier to criticize ourselves than to love ourselves. And yet, self-criticism can be damaging, leading to a negative self-image and a lack of self-compassion. You may harshly judge yourself for mistakes or perceived flaws, leading to feelings of shame or guilt. These patterns of self-doubt and self-criticism can hold you back from achieving your full potential and living a fulfilling life. Recognizing and addressing these tendencies is vital to building a strong sense of self-worth and self-identity. But why is it so hard? Well, because loving ourselves and trusting ourselves requires **real work**, and that's hard to do.

What does that *real work* entail? It starts with **self-awareness**. It's about understanding our thoughts, emotions, and behaviors because it helps us recognize our strengths and weaknesses, guiding us to make decisions. It's also about showing *reliability* and *consistency* in our actions and decisions. This builds our self-confidence and reinforces our trust in our ability to handle whatever challenges are in our way *effectively*.

It's about focusing on our previous **positive experiences** because our past successes contribute to believing in our capabilities, creating trust in our problem-solving skills and decision-making process. We start trusting that we *know* what we are doing and slowly eliminate feelings of "imposter syndrome." Of course, that also means we need **self-compassion** because treating ourselves with kindness and understanding, especially during times of failure or mistake, promotes a forgiving attitude. This also makes it easier to trust our future decisions.

Finally, we need to **reflect** because it allows us to learn from our failures and successes, which makes it possible for us to grow and adapt. Adaptability is the most coveted of skills in all areas of life. The one who can adapt will always survive.

Indeed, a strong sense of self-love and self-worth clearly conveys that you believe you deserve the best in life. It is a promise you make to yourself, telling yourself that you will respect and love yourself, no matter what. This attracts situations and people who recognize and appreciate your worth, leading to healthier relationships and opportunities.

But self-love goes *beyond* just that. It encourages positive self-talk and affirmations. You're more likely to use empowering language and thoughts when you love yourself, and positive self-talk can reprogram your subconscious to support all your desires. Love yourself deeply!

Self-love is essential to self-care. Taking care of your physical, emotional, and mental well-being is necessary for a positive outlook on life and a happy disposition. Just think about how you feel when you haven't exercised in a while, haven't showered, or been eating well. You *know* you don't feel so great about your choices, so you enter a vicious cycle that makes you feel worse and worse until you say, "That's enough!" This is why we need to prioritize self-care – it involves mental and physical changes that can help you look and feel better inside *and* outside.

Indeed, developing self-love can provide inner strength and resilience, which are crucial when overcoming challenges and setbacks. When you have faith in yourself, you are more likely to bounce back from difficulties and continue pursuing your goals. It makes you feel capable of *anything* you set your mind to – and there's no more incredible feeling than that.

Embrace All Sides of Yourself and Your Life

No, you aren't perfect, but that's also a side to yourself that you *should* love. Our imperfections are part of our individuality and charm. Recognizing and embracing our imperfections helps us to foster self-compassion and diminishes self-criticism. Sure, you can occasionally be slightly critical of yourself and be self-**aware** of your faults but

don't focus on the flaws. Don't engage in a cycle of *constantly* criticizing yourself!

Recognizing when something doesn't align with your needs would be best. This means setting up appropriate boundaries. Establishing **clear boundaries** with others protects our energy and well-being, reinforcing our self-respect and self-worth. Learn to say no when needed and if it conflicts with prioritizing your needs. Yes, you **can** say no.

Life's too short to do boring things. Find and engage in activities that make you happy. Actively seeking out and participating in things that bring us joy helps to nurture a positive sense of self and enhances our overall well-being. It gives us something fun to do and something fun to talk about. It *adds* value to a well-rounded life.

Finally, *commit* to personal development and learning from experiences. Embracing growth encourages us to step out of our comfort zones, learn from our mistakes, and appreciate our journey toward becoming our best selves. This is where the *real growth* starts to happen!

Ultimately, when you love and value yourself, you **open up to receiving more of everything** in various forms, including financial success, opportunities, and happiness. It helps you clarify your desires and intentions. You know what you want, and *you start* looking for ways to get it. That sure beats feeling like you aren't good enough or like you will never reach your goals. That's why you need to put your self-love above all else! Practicing self-love allows you to experience and understand the concept of *unconditional* love. *Self-love is self-care.*

Some tips and techniques for practicing self-care:

1. Take 30 deep breaths, filling your lungs entirely and releasing each breath slowly. This has a calming effect and also helps boost your oxygen levels.

2. Write down three things you appreciate about yourself and practice self-compassion by offering yourself words of encouragement and understanding. Be gentle with yourself.

3. Spend a few moments reminding yourself of things you like about yourself. Use positive statements, such as "I am worthy," or "I love myself just as I am," or "I am enough."

4. Take a nice hot shower or soak in a bath, focusing on letting the water relax you.

5. Hydrate. Drink lots of water. Water is essential for various bodily functions like regulating body temperature, lubricating joints, aiding digestion, flushing out the liver and kidneys, and carrying nutrients and oxygen to cells.[4] Not to mention what it does for your skin and complexion. It can also help support weight management. Sometimes, feeling thirsty can be mistaken for hunger, and we reach for little snacky snacks instead of water.

6. Do any physical activity you enjoy, whether a brisk walk, yoga session, or dance workout, to boost your mood and energy levels.

7. Get some sunshine every day. Morning light is best, but any amount of time outdoors is good. Get at least 10 minutes but try for 20-30 minutes if possible. Sunlight is essential for vitamin D production[5], supporting bone health and immune function. Sunlight also helps regulate mood by stimulating serotonin production and maintains a healthy sleep-wake cycle by regulating the circadian rhythm.

---

[4] https://www.hsph.harvard.edu/news/hsph-in-the-news/the-importance-of-hydration/.
[5] https://www.ncbi.nlm.nih.gov/pmc/articles/PMC10239563/#:~:text=UV%20exposure%20is%20the%20primary,absorption%20and%20vitamin%20D%20production.

8. Treat yourself with kindness and compassion by prioritizing your needs and desires.

9. Engage in activities that bring you joy and fulfillment without guilt or judgment, whether reading a book, spending time with friends, walking in nature, or pursuing a hobby you love.

10. Practice the Italian saying, "Dolce far niente," which translates to "the sweetness of doing nothing." Sometimes, the most revolutionary self-care technique is doing NOTHING. This allows for relaxation, reflection, and rejuvenation. Taking breaks from the busyness of life gives your mind and body a chance to rest and recharge. It can help reduce stress levels, improve mental clarity, and promote overall well-being. It's powerful to give yourself permission, allowing yourself the gift of stillness. View these moments of doing nothing as opportunities for inner peace. Be present in the moment and give yourself the chance to pause. Simply enjoy life. Let the world spin on without you for a little while.

When you learn to perfect this set of techniques, you begin to value and love yourself more profoundly. You will start treating yourself with the same care and affection you would give to any other significant person in your life. We tend to be kind and forgiving towards others, but we often neglect to extend the same kindness to ourselves. And yet, we are stuck with ourselves for life! So why is it *so hard* to be kind?!

We often reserve our best efforts and time for others, and this is a habit we have to learn to extend to ourselves. It is crucial to embrace and cherish yourself and prioritize self-love above everything else. While the information in this guide may be helpful, if you only take away one thing, please let it be the importance of loving yourself. Remember that you are worthy of love and respect. I urge you to try treating yourself with kindness and compassion.

1. I love and accept myself unconditionally.

2. My self-love nurtures and heals me.

3. I am enough just as I am.

4. I am deserving of all good things.

5. I am special.

6. I am worthy.

7. I forgive myself for any past mistakes and release all judgment.

8. My self-love grows stronger with each passing day.

9. I am confident.

10. I radiate love and compassion to myself and others.

Chapter Ten

—•◯•—

Attracting Love

L ove is a vital and fundamental human need. Whether we want to admit it or not, it's something we all want. Sure, you might be telling people you are an "Independent Queen or King," but you likely still crave love deep down. We look for it and find it in different forms. From friends. From family. From our pets. And yes, maybe even from a romantic relationship. It's okay to admit that we like feeling loved. It's just a part of how humans are wired. Let's have a look at why.

Love Is a Basic Need

It is often said that "all we need is love." Well, maybe not ALL, but it is pretty darn important to our existence! Ask anyone who has ever felt unloved about the despair that it brings. It seems that we are wired to try and belong. Love and belonging are crucial components of Maslow's hierarchy of human needs.[6] Being loved is a precursor that must be met for individuals seeking to realize their full potential, pursue personal growth, and achieve self-fulfillment. Individuals typically progress through the hierarchy in a sequential manner, starting with fulfilling basic needs before moving to higher-level needs. This is why attracting love and nurturing loving relationships contribute significantly to your emotional well-being and happiness.

There are many reasons we crave love. There are biological, psychological, evolutionary survival & neuro-chemical dimensions

---

[6] Maslow, A. H. (1943). A theory of human motivation. Psychological Review, 50 (4), 370-96.

of love.[7] Love is kind and patient and all that is good about humanity. It is an incomparable feeling, and our ability to express, feel, and share love is a defining characteristic of humanity. I personally would argue that it is the best part of living. But love is not only about *romantic* love. Many don't allow themselves to see the **love that is all around them.** Love is so often found in the embrace of our families, friendships, and self.

Love generates positive energy. When you have loving and harmonious relationships, you emit happiness, joy, and serenity that align with positivity and abundance. This positive energy attracts more joyful experiences and opportunities into your life.

The process of attracting love often involves self-love and self-acceptance. Before attracting a loving partner or loving relationship, you may need to work on self-worth and self-esteem. As discussed in the previous chapter, self-love must be a priority as it enhances your happiness and positively impacts other areas of your life!

Attracting love also encourages you to focus on healthy and positive relationships. These relationships can provide support, encouragement, and inspiration, further enhancing your life. On the other hand, attracting a negative or harmful kind of love – the toxic kind – can do the opposite: it can completely break you. The damage that comes from toxic love can take years to undo. This is why you need self-love – to know **how you want to be treated** and the kind of treatment **you absolutely do not allow**. It is much easier to never engage in toxic relationships than it is to extricate yourself from one or recover from surviving one.

Love Can Be Inspiring

Love can also be a motivating and inspiring force. Being in a loving relationship can inspire you to reach for your goals and dreams with incredible determination and passion, leading to expanded success.

---

[7] Fisher, H. (2004). Why We Love: The Nature and Chemistry of Romantic Love. New York, NY: Macmillan.

We often do our best to look our best, be our best, and stay healthy and active when we feel loved or have self-love because love *inspires us* to be the best version of ourselves.

Love is also a powerful emotion that radiates outward. When you attract love, you often experience an expansion of love in other aspects of your life. This includes self-love, love for others, and love for life itself. So, you feel like rays of support and positivity surround you. Who wouldn't want that?!

Likewise, successfully attracting love can strengthen your belief system. When you see your intentions in the form of a loving relationship, you gain confidence in your ability to achieve your other desires. It brings joy and fulfillment into your life. These positive emotions are essential for maintaining a mindset of positivity and happiness. We *all* want love in one way or another!

Changing Your Beliefs About Love

Before looking at methods to attract love, you must identify any limiting beliefs blocking you from finding love. Some common limiting beliefs include: "I'm not attractive enough," "I'm too old to find love," and "I always attract the wrong kind of people."

Once you've identified your limiting beliefs, create positive affirmations that counter them. For example, if your limiting belief is "I'm not attractive enough," your affirmation could be "I am beautiful and deserving of love." Make sure your affirmations are framed in a positive tone. Try to use the present tense when creating them and speaking the words out loud.

Here are some tips you can implement to attract love and help you to be more open to love:

<u>Friendships:</u>

1. Be Authentic. Show up as your true self and be genuine in your interactions. Authenticity fosters trust and connections in friendships.

2. Be a Good Listener: Practice active listening and show genuine interest in others' lives. Being a supportive and empathetic friend strengthens bonds and cultivates lasting friendships.
3. Initiate Plans. Take the initiative to plan outings or activities with friends. Proactive efforts to spend quality time together nurture friendships and create cherished memories.

Family:

1. Prioritize Quality Time. Make time for meaningful interactions with family members. Whether sharing a meal together or participating in family traditions, quality time strengthens familial bonds.
2. Express Gratitude. Show appreciation for your family members and express gratitude for the love and support they provide. Small gestures of thanks go a long way in nurturing family relationships.
3. Set Boundaries. Establish healthy boundaries with family members to maintain harmony and respect within each relationship. Clear communication about individual needs and expectations can prevent a lot of hurt feelings and misunderstandings along the way.

Romantic Love:

1. Know Your Worth. Recognize your own value and worthiness of love and respect in relationships. Set high standards for how you deserve to be treated, and don't settle for anything less.
2. Let Go of Past Baggage. Release any lingering hurt or resentment from past relationships. Holding onto negative emotions can block you from being open to new love. Embrace forgiveness and move forward with a clean slate. This gift you give yourself is not to release the other person from the responsibility they hold. It is to remove the grip- that holding the pain they caused- has on you. It is not about them.

3. Get Out There (Literally). Love is not going to show up on your doorstep (unless it's a particularly romantic delivery person). Expand your social circle and engage in activities you enjoy. Whether it's joining a club, attending events, or trying out new hobbies, being proactive in meeting new people increases your chances of finding someone compatible. Get on the Apps if that is something you would consider.

4. Practice Vulnerability. Allow yourself to be vulnerable and authentic in your interactions with others. Opening up emotionally fosters depth in connections and creates space for love to flourish.

5. You're a catch, so own it! Be your fabulous self. Confidence is magnetic, and besides, who wants to be with someone who doesn't appreciate your fantastic quirks?

6. Keep an Open Mind. Be receptive to meeting people from different backgrounds and with varied interests. Love can sometimes come in unexpected packages, so remain open to exploring connections with a diverse range of individuals.

7. Stay Present. Focus on the present moment rather than worrying about the future or dwelling on the past. Being mindful allows you to fully experience and appreciate the opportunities for love that come your way.

8. Follow Your Heart: Listen to your intuition and trust your instincts when it comes to matters of the heart. Allow yourself to follow the path that feels right for you, even if it diverges from your original plans or expectations.

9. Flash those pearly whites! Wear a smile on your face as often as possible. Smiles are inviting and infectious in a good way! A smile is the universal language of love, plus it's free.

10. Be Patient and Persistent: Understand that finding love takes time and effort. Be patient with yourself and others, and don't get discouraged by setbacks or rejections. Stay persistent in your pursuit of love, knowing the right person is out there waiting for you.

11. Sprinkle kindness like confetti everywhere you go! You never know what next kind gesture will lead to something more or get you noticed.

12. Don't Take Yourself Too Seriously: Laughter is the best aphrodisiac! Keep it light, crack a joke, and remember that finding love is supposed to be fun and light, not feel like work. Plus, who doesn't love someone who can make them laugh?

13. Communicate Clearly: Be open and honest about your intentions and desires. Effective communication fosters understanding, paving the way for meaningful relationships to blossom. Feel free to express yourself authentically and listen actively to others.

Remember that love should be natural, effortless, and never feel forced or laborious. It should flow easily to and from you.

By opening your heart to love, you can improve your relationships and attract meaningful, long-lasting connections into your life.

Remember to allow others to love you. You have to be open and receptive to allow love in. What a warm, uplifting, and priceless gift to give our spirit!

1. I am open to receiving love in many forms.

2. I attract healthy and loving relationships.

3. I deserve to be respected and cherished.

4. Love flows to me from all directions.

5. My heart is ready to give and receive love.

6. I deserve loving and fulfilling relationships.

7. I radiate love and attract it in return.

8. I release any past heartaches and am open to new love.

9. I am a magnet for deep and meaningful connections.

10. Love comes to me effortlessly and easily.

Chapter Eleven

———•◯•———

Healthy Eating

The dreaded food chapter. Food is complex. Food is not just about calories in and calories out. And yet, if you've often struggled with your relationship with food, you know *all too well* the power that food can have over you. Let's look at what healthy eating *really is* and what it is *not*.

A Healthy Relationship with Food

A healthy relationship with food is crucial to achieving physical well-being. This is because your food choices and relationship with food significantly impact your emotional well-being. A healthy relationship with food can reduce stress, anxiety, and negative emotions associated with food and eating. This doesn't mean being in control of what you eat 100% of the time. Food is **fuel**. It's how you make your body *feel good*. If it takes up all your mental space, I am sorry to say – you don't have a healthy relationship with food. I definitely didn't for years.

It's essential to recognize that how you treat your body, including your dietary choices, influences your mind-body connection. You promote physical and mental well-being by nourishing your body with enough wholesome and nutritious food choices. But the opposite is also true!

A healthy body and mind are more receptive to positive energy, and you tend to have more energy to do what you need to achieve your goals. Staying fit helps your mobility and allows you to do more and quite literally be able to go more places. It allows you to get more done, leading to more efficiency and less stress.

As someone who has struggled with weight for most of my life and experienced a sense of deep dread at the mere thought of exercise, I understand the struggle to find a healthy relationship with food and movement. For most of my adult life, I have found myself between 50 and 275- pounds overweight. When I was at my highest weight and lowest emotional point, I weighed in at just over 400 pounds— 404 pounds, to be exact. I know these numbers look like typos, computer errors, and area codes; they are so large. The numbers still shock even me, especially to see them in print. I almost left this section out as it requires allowing this vulnerability to be put out there for onslaught. Even today, as I type this, I immediately feel a pang of shame surface. But it is a real part of what sparked this need to reset my mindset. So here we are, baring and sharing my most difficult truths.

Throughout my life, there have been a series of unfortunate events. There has been so much loss. My father's death, when he was just 49 years old, was monumental. Cancer swept through my father's side of the family like a plague, claiming so many on that side of the family tree. People I loved and that mattered to me deeply. My husband's battle with cancer and subsequent death was also traumatic for both my children and me. That time of my life could be its own book. The toll was physical and mental. **Grief and loss do terrible things to our psyche**. Watching my sister battle cancer and being so helpless to do anything about it was also emotionally devastating and drained my mental reserves. I had my own medical binder's worth of health issues as well. My own battles with cancer. There were so many medical procedures, treatments, and surgeries. I survived, luckily, but I had to part with over 10 organs/body parts in exchange for the right to be here still. I have lost count of the exact number and try not to think about it too often. All of this certainly contributed to my weight gain and struggles. But while these factors had an enormous impact on my physical (and mental) health, another reason for being overweight for so much of my life is that I loved food. I loved everything about food: cooking it and the social aspects involving going out to eat and celebrating everything with food. I come from a family where **food is "comfort."** It is how we show love. We feed everyone. If you are around us for more than 2 minutes, you will be offered something to eat, and if you refuse, that's ok, but we will still cook for you and offer you not one but several choices to choose from. My parents owned coffee shops and diners and were fabulous chefs. I started cooking at my mother's side when I was six years old. I worked alongside them at the family business at the age of 13, and that is when I gained my first big chunk of weight, pushing me from what would be considered normal to chubby. Over the years, **chubby escalated to obese** pretty steadily. I have always used food to *fill voids and bring happiness*. I used my personality and humor as tools to cope and project an ease and confidence I didn't always feel inside.

Even though I was overweight most of my life, I was never a person who didn't care for herself at all. I *always* made every effort to look put together. I always had my hair, makeup, and nails done. Looking neat, tidy, and well put together was incredibly important to me. I wanted to make sure that I looked good and that I looked *polished*. The reason for the emphasis is that I knew I would **immediately be judged by my size**, so I had to make sure all the stereotypes and preconceptions would be dismissed as I hit all the other targets that might be aimed my way due to my size.

I am also obsessive about hygiene, showering 2-3 times daily for the same reasons. I must always be the best-smelling person in a room. Smelling delicious is a part of my personal brand! I spent a fortune on plus-size clothing and accessories to look as put together as possible in the oversized body I had *created*.

I took so much time and effort to look as good as possible within the confines of the body that I had trapped myself in. No one ever believed me when we talked about what I weighed because I used every trick in the book not to look like what I weighed. Clothing color, styles, angles, and anything that could create an illusion of being smaller. Life would have been much easier if I had only applied those efforts and time to get healthier sooner.

Take this as you would the advice given by your older sister: you can care about how you look even when you aren't taking all the steps needed to fulfill what you want to look like in the end. And, if you've never been overweight, please note that most overweight people aren't lazy! We probably take more steps dealing with workarounds about our weight than you can imagine. We don't all lack self-discipline in all areas. Everyone has problems, and mine were just easier to see when someone met me – I overate. But I had to deal with the consequences of doing this to myself until I decided *enough was enough*.

But making the change wasn't easy *at all*. Throughout my life, I've dieted off and on. I tried every diet that you can imagine. Every fad diet and every nutrition plan doctors and nutritionists recommend. I tried acupuncture, Keto, Paleo, Beach diets, liquid diets, Cabbage soup, Carnivore diets, all the big commercial diets and prepared meal plans, and intermittent fasting. You get the idea… I tried many times. I probably dieted most of my adult life. I would get on the **diet hamster wheel**, lose a bit of weight, and then proceed to **gain it back with interest accrued** each time.

I was never full, no matter how much I ate. My attitude turned to thinking that if I was going to be fat, I might as well enjoy it. This was just a ruse, permitting myself to eat more of the caloric foods I liked vs. the foods I should be eating. That is until I was forced to take measures due to the reappearance of cancer.

I knew that **if I wanted to live**, I had to get myself into a healthier mindset and *do it quickly*. With this wake-up call and shift in mindset, I dropped the first 150-plus pounds of weight. I achieved significant weight loss with the help of medical professionals. I underwent a hysterectomy, partial removal of my stomach, and reduction of liver size through diet and increased exercise, calorie deficits, and other healthier lifestyle choices. The most significant difference was that I started moving my body more, eating less, and choosing healthier, more filling options.

I started walking for tiny amounts of time, just one minute a day, and gradually increased the duration by one minute each day. Eventually, I could walk for 30, 60, and even 100 minutes a day. I no longer require knee surgery. I feel happier and more excited about being outside in the sun and taking walks or running errands, something I used to dread because it hurt so much that *I would cry daily*. Now, the only tears I shed being active are tears of joy because *I feel so free* and mobile. I now look forward to events and more physical activities. I have changed the way I see things. This **shift in perspective** doesn't allow me to see these new habits as restrictive, painful, or a chore. I am *so happy* to take these steps that are good for my body. Whenever I say no to something I know will make me feel worse later, I have a huge sense of pride and accomplishment. I **choose** to do things differently.

Today, I still eat everything I love, but usually healthier versions of what I used to eat. I now eat more moderate, mindful portions. With this mindset change, I look forward to cooking and eating just as much as I used to. The difference is that I think of food in a healthier way now.

With the actions I was taking, steadily and surely, the weight came off. I continue on this path as I deal with the rest of the pounds that need to be shed. I recognize that it is a mindset I will have to continue practicing. It is a lifestyle choice now.

It is not always easy. Even after victories, we still have to deal with the fallout from our battles. After surgery, I would look at myself in the mirror and sob uncontrollably. Staring in the mirror at the stitched scar lines, put back together like a patchwork quilt. I was giving off "Frankenstein" vibes *after* each surgery. I had a hard time loving myself, or more explicitly loving how I looked, and it took over other parts of my life, too. It's tough to love yourself when you create a body that doesn't fit what society expects of you.

But now, things have changed. I have **learned to love myself as I am**, *scars and all*. Now, I trace those lines on the scars and love every part of them as they are hard proof that *I survived everything* that tried to kill me! I see them as little victory notches that make me feel **badass**! Perhaps you have your own marks on your body that show *your* story, too. Mothers often have stretch marks as reminders or souvenirs of the children they bore. As we age, we all have wrinkles and smile lines, which should *remind us* that we have *lived and laughed*.

We should embrace the evidence left behind by our experiences and not use them as weapons to beat ourselves down.

Take Good Care of Yourself!

Practicing mindful eating and making healthy food choices is a form of self-care. It demonstrates self-love and self-respect. When you prioritize self-care, you send a powerful message to everyone and everything around you that you value yourself and your well-being.

Unhealthy eating habits, such as overindulging in processed or unhealthy foods, can make you feel weighed down. These foods may lead to feelings of sluggishness, guilt, or discomfort. On the other hand, mainly consuming healthy food throughout the day can enhance your energy levels, uplift your mood, and improve your overall wellness.

A healthy diet often aligns with your intentions for well-being, vitality, and longevity. When you eat nourishing foods, you support your body's **optimal functioning**. You are basically giving your cells the nutrients they need to work best. This can also make you feel emotionally *lighter*.

Unhealthy eating habits can create resistance within you, leading to inner conflict and negative energy. For example, suppose you have guilt or shame associated with your food choices. In that case, it can hinder your ability to do anything positively because of the negativity these feelings bring. Embracing a healthy relationship with food reduces this resistance and allows everything, including you, to move more freely.

Likewise, a healthy mindset about food can lead to improved body confidence and self-esteem. When you feel good about your body, you radiate self-assuredness, and your happiness is evident to everyone, including you. People are always telling me that I am *glowing* these days. It is such a wonderful compliment to hear. I light up even more every time I hear it; it will **never** get old!

Making the Right Choices

Many of us tend to eat for emotional reasons or out of boredom rather than because of actual hunger – we don't make *mindful* choices. Developing new coping mechanisms that address the root cause of our emotionally driven eating habits is crucial to tackling this issue. It's worth investing the time and effort in exploring healthy ways to cope, and please don't hesitate to seek professional help if needed.

Keep in mind that **developing new habits takes time.** Be gentle with yourself and have patience and resilience. You can have a bad day or even a bad week; it's ok. Start again at the next meal. Don't beat yourself up. *Just move forward.* Your past thinking, processes, and actions have nothing new to offer you, so be present and take the next steps to make yourself feel better. Each time you make a better choice, your feeling of accomplishment will be worth the effort.

Choosing to eat in a healthy and mindful way requires a certain amount of **self-discipline**. Exercising self-discipline in one area of our lives can spill over into other areas, helping us stay focused on our intentions and goals.

We have the power to shape the choices we make and adjust our attitudes towards food. It's crucial to let go of limiting beliefs we might hold about food and try new things. Being adventurous opens us up to a broader range of choices!

Cultivating a positive and healthy relationship with what you eat is very important. Eating is not bad; there are no bad foods, just bad food *choices*. We need food to survive and live comfortable and satisfying lives. It's perfectly normal to enjoy food and all that surrounds eating. We should not always deprive ourselves of foods that are considered unhealthy. Instead, we should learn to enjoy what we eat in moderation and in a way that *supports our bodies* rather than adding strain and stress to them.

Adopting healthy eating habits requires a mindful approach and practical strategies that align with your lifestyle and preferences. You can start by pre-planning your meals so that each one is balanced and has enough of what your body needs to be fueled. This means choosing well-rounded meals that are easy to prepare and include foods that you will actually want to eat. It also means focusing on portion control and recognizing when your body is full.

Another way to achieve a healthy diet mindset is to romanticize your meals. You can enhance your experience by presenting your food on fine or fun plates and arranging it beautifully. This way, all your senses will be satisfied, and your experience will be more fulfilling.

Be in Tune with Your Body

It's essential to be in tune with our body's hunger and fullness signals and listen to what it tells us. We should respect our body and the messages it sends us. Take the time to enjoy and savor your food, allowing yourself to become more in sync with your eating habits. Please slow down and appreciate each bite, allowing your body to recognize when it is *full*. Sometimes, it can take a few minutes for our "feeling full" signals to **catch up to the speed of our forks**.

A healthy diet contributes to your overall well-being, including physical health, mental clarity, and emotional stability.

Your body is beautiful and has carried you this far; it has gotten you through all your bad, good and just ok days, so *be nice to it*.

I urge you to try to take care of the original equipment! Spare parts are hard to come by; take it from someone who knows.

1. I am in control of my eating habits and make wise choices.

2. I make healthy and nourishing food choices.

3. I listen to my body and eat only when hungry.

4. I enjoy the flavors of healthy foods and feel satisfied with them.

5. My body deserves to be nourished with wholesome and nutritious foods.

6. I savor every bite of my meals and eat mindfully.

7. I am attuned to my body's hunger and fullness cues.

8. Cravings for unhealthy foods are fading away.

9. I am mindful of portion sizes and eat in moderation.

10. My body is worthy, and I treat it with love and respect.

Chapter Twelve

———•◉•———

Ensuring a Good Night's Sleep

Quality sleep is **not** a luxury; it's a fundamental pillar of overall health and happiness. I bet you feel the difference when you have a great night's sleep and when you don't! Perhaps you're grumpier and snappier or wake up wishing you could stay in bed all day. This chapter will explore the significant impact of quality sleep on our physical, emotional, and mental health.

My Sleep Journey

For years, I struggled to sleep more than a few hours, enduring the consequences of restless nights without taking proactive steps to address the issue. The toll it took on my body and mind was undeniable, yet I found myself making excuses rather than seeking solutions.

I managed to function for years at this crazy pace of long hours with little sleep but at a tremendous cost to my body and health. Your body will remember everything you do to it and for it. If you don't take the time to rest on a regular schedule, trust me, you will be forced to make the time later to heal from the effects of the exhaustion.

The transformation was remarkable once I committed to prioritizing my sleep. I now make sure I am getting at least 6 hours every night. Although it is interrupted, I ensure I return to bed and sleep. It took some time to build up to 6 hours, and I aim for 7 whenever possible. I discovered firsthand the life-changing benefits of adequate rest. It really *is* rejuvenating! I feel better, have more energy, am no longer tired all the time, and, as a bonus, the brain fog has lifted.

A good night's sleep enhances our mood and cognitive function, reduces stress, and improves our resilience. Quality sleep plays a significant role in developing emotional resilience, helping you bounce back from setbacks and challenges more easily. However, getting restful sleep is not just about the number of hours we sleep; it also involves cultivating healthy sleep habits and addressing any underlying factors affecting our sleep patterns.

When you get a good night's sleep and wake up feeling refreshed, you are simply in a better mood. You're in a mindset conducive to attracting positive experiences and interactions. Your energy reserves have been replenished, so you have a spring in your step as you face the day. On the other hand, we have all experienced sleep that left us wanting more, and let's just say that those aren't our best days!

The Science Behind Sleep

Quality sleep enhances mental clarity and cognitive function[8]. You can better set clear intentions when your mind is clear and focused. Likewise, sleep is crucial for emotional regulation. Lack of sleep can cause mood swings, irritability, and stress. How often do we get what we want when miserable and grumpy? The answer is likely not too often. How often do we get what we want done when smiling and looking forward to it? A lot more often, I bet! So, rest is an integral part of being in a good mood. If you are too tired to focus, you are not productive and cannot do your best at anything. So, get some rest!

Getting a good night's sleep is crucial for managing stress and anxiety. Stress, left unchecked, can dampen creativity and positivity. Yet adequate sleep acts as a buffer, promoting relaxation and emotional equilibrium and reducing the detrimental effects of stress. Sleep is essential for optimal bodily function, replenishing energy reserves, and boosting the vitality you need to navigate life's demands and responsibilities.

---

[8]https://www.health.harvard.edu/mind-and-mood/sharpen-thinking-skills-with-a-better-nights-
sleep#:~:text=Getting%20more%20sleep%20can%20help,may%20be%20the%20key%20word.

REM[9] (rapid eye movement) sleep is particularly significant, characterized by vivid dreams and profound creative insights. During REM sleep, the brain consolidates memories, processes emotions, and synthesizes new ideas. The dreams we dream during this time offer invaluable guidance and inspiration. When we recall these dreams, we can use the ideas inspired during our restful state to do things that result in personal growth and tackle problem-solving. By aligning our sleep patterns with the body's natural circadian rhythms, we can harness the power of REM sleep to nurture creativity and promote overall well-being, ensuring we awaken refreshed, revitalized, and ready to seize the day.

Let's take a look at some easy ways you can start to improve your sleep habits:

1. Establish a Consistent Sleep Schedule
2. Create a Relaxing Bedtime Routine
3. Optimize Your Sleep Environment
4. Limit Screen Time Before Bed
5. Practice Bedtime Affirmations

If you suspect you are deficient in essential vitamins and nutrients, consult your doctor to see if supplements can help. This was an issue for me; my vitamin D3 and cortisol levels inhibited my ability to get quality sleep. I was also advised to use a magnesium supplement. These imbalances can impact your body's metabolism and rhythms, making it difficult to unwind and maintain a healthy sleep cycle. Don't hesitate to consult a medical professional for advice on improving your sleep patterns.

To ensure your body functions correctly during waking and resting hours, prioritize getting enough sleep. Don't let the little things you can easily change and fix wreak havoc on your body's functions during waking hours. Get your "ZZZS" in and be gentle with yourself as you unwind for the night.

---

[9]https://my.clevelandclinic.org/health/body/12148-sleep-basics#:~:text=Rapid%20eye%20movement%20(REM)%20sleep%20is%20the%20stage%20of%20sleep,of%20your%20total%20time%20asleep.

1. I allow myself to relax deeply as I prepare for sleep.

2. My bedroom is a sanctuary of rest and rejuvenation.

3. Every night, I fall asleep easily and sleep soundly.

4. I release all worries and stress from the day.

5. Sleep comes to me naturally and effortlessly.

6. My body and mind are in perfect harmony for sleep.

7. I am grateful for the restorative sleep I receive each night.

8. I let go of any tension in my body and drift into peaceful slumber.

9. My dreams are positive and full of serenity.

10. I wake up each morning feeling refreshed and energized.

Chapter Thirteen

---•◯•---

Opportunities

"Carpe Diem!"

Life is a treasure trove of opportunities just waiting to be seized. Often, these golden chances align perfectly with our desires and goals, offering a pathway to achievement. Attracting and taking these opportunities draws you closer to the desired outcomes. So, keep your eyes peeled, stay sharp, stay attuned, and be ready to pounce when those opportunities come knocking. Timing is everything, and chances don't usually wait around while you decide if you will take them.

Let's actively embrace opportunities, take decisive action, and cultivate a mindset that attracts and capitalizes on the chances presented. And don't worry; I've got a few helpful strategies to help you navigate these opportunities like a pro.

You Need to Take Action!

Taking advantage of opportunities requires action. It means *actively* working towards your goals and aligning your actions with your intentions. Seizing one opportunity can set off an avalanche of possibilities. Think of a snowball rolling down a mountain, gaining momentum and propelling progress forward, leading to quicker results. The first opportunity can branch off into a limitless number of offshoots and consequent possibilities to act upon. So, work on chances to get them started.

Seize the Moment

Don't let opportunities pass you by; research and learn what you need to know to make the decisions that will improve your life. To effectively seize opportunities, remain **proactive** and open-minded, seek avenues aligned with goals and aspirations, and stay informed about emerging trends and potential opportunities in your field. Building connections through networking with like-minded individuals can often lead to prospects and fruitful partnerships.

Keep Learning

I've said it before, and I'll say it again. Continuous learning is crucial for staying adaptable, as knowledge is a powerful tool that helps you identify and capitalize on opportunities. The more you learn, the easier it will become to **identify things others do not see**. You will start to build an impressive information database in your mind. As you do this, you will become **more aware of patterns and notice little trends before others** do. This ability becomes a superpower to allow you to take full advantage of opportunities. Learn to recognize these chances for both personal and professional growth.

Challenges Will Come – Get Back Up!

Yes, challenges will come by. Yes, you'll probably face hard times in your journey. What will you do about it? Will you give up, or will you get back up? Adaptability and resilience are *key* to success, maximizing potential options, and overcoming challenges. Challenges are inevitable on the path to success, but they can be overcome with the right mindset and strategies. See every obstacle as a fortuitous redirection to do more and better things. Reframe setbacks as learning opportunities and develop resilience to bounce back stronger. Success is not just about luck; it requires preparation, perseverance, and a willingness to adapt.

You're Not Alone

You're not alone in this. You don't need to do it all on your own. So, seek guidance from experienced individuals who have navigated similar challenges, as learning from others' experiences can provide valuable insights and strategies. Ask for advice and reach out to your network of friends, colleagues, and peers for support and direction. We have more resources at our disposal than we realize.

Don't Overwhelm Yourself

Maybe things get complicated. Maybe things might get tricky. Don't just give up because you *can* make things easier for yourself. Deconstruct larger challenges into smaller, more manageable tasks and focus on taking one step at a time to maintain momentum and avoid feeling overwhelmed.

Believe!

Confidence grows with each chance acted upon, enhancing your options and ability to achieve successful outcomes. Stay persistent. A good old-fashioned stubborn streak can be helpful in sticking to the plan. Keep the faith!

Look for opportunities in things that are interesting to you, that matter to you, and that you are passionate about. Exploring those paths or aims will bring you the most satisfaction and joy. Anytime you do something you enjoy it feels like fun instead of a chore or bore. Enjoying what you do also helps you believe this is the right moment for you!

Get Past Your Fear

Fear can be crippling to momentum. Be courageous and remove limiting beliefs that cause you fear or doubt. Do enough research to feel confident climbing the ladder rungs of the opportunities you choose to explore.

Don't let setbacks deter, deflate, or derail you; instead, let them be the *motivation or power* that drives and fuels your *passion forward*. Rise above the naysayers; when they try to bring you down, show them they've only **fueled the flames of your determination** even higher.

Remember that success is within reach when you keep your mind sharp, stay on your toes, and take those opportunities like a master chess player strategizing their next move. **You've got the smarts required to make it happen!**

1. Opportunities come to me in perfect timing.

2. Every day brings new chances for growth and success.

3. I am open to opportunities that align with my goals.

4. Opportunities flow to me effortlessly and abundantly.

5. I am a magnet for opportunities that elevate my life.

6. I recognize and seize opportunities with confidence.

7. My mindset is attuned to recognizing opportunities.

8. I am in the right place at the right time for opportunities.

9. I welcome opportunities as the keys to my success.

10. I am a proactive creator of opportunities in my life.

Chapter Fourteen

———•◯•———

The Transformative Power of Gratitude

I n today's world, it's easy to get caught up in the pursuit of more – more success, more possessions, and more experiences. However, what if the key to a fulfilling and abundant life lies not in pursuing more but in appreciating what we already have? This is the essence of gratitude. When you sprinkle gratitude into your daily routine, you shift your focus from what's lacking to the abundance around you. It's like having a lens that magnifies the positive, turning ordinary moments into extraordinary blessings. Let's look at the great things gratitude can do for you!

Gratitude: A Life Hack

Living with gratitude is the shortcut to an effortless and happy life, as it transforms challenges into opportunities for appreciation and cultivates a mindset where every day feels easy and full.

Gratitude is the simple act of acknowledging and appreciating the big and small "blessings" surrounding you. It is more than a polite platitude. Gratitude is not only saying "thank you" when someone holds the door for you or hands you a gift. It's a mindset, a way of life, and a path to happiness.

Gratitude is **transformative** because it shifts your perspective from scarcity to abundance. Rather than focusing on what you lack, you begin to see the richness of your life. It can be as simple as the roof over your head, clean water, a mess to clean made by happy children, or food in your belly—family, friends, a job, and all the other little things we take for granted. Taking the time to acknowledge and recognize just how much abundance we already have is humbling, and the internal brain shift happens almost immediately.

Show Gratitude for Others

Expressing gratitude towards others strengthens your relationships. It fosters trust, kindness, and love. Gratitude has even been linked to improved mental well-being, reducing stress, depression, and anxiety, and promoting happiness. When we express gratitude, our brains release feel-good neurotransmitters like dopamine and serotonin. The release of more of those happy chemicals brings us an immediate rush of happiness and contentment. If you feel like your relationships are struggling, take some time to think about why you are grateful for them. This alone can help shift your mindset! Practicing gratitude can also help you cope with challenges more effectively by reminding you of your inner strength and the support you have.

Gratitude as a Magnet

When you appreciate what you have, you attract more of it. Gratitude is a magnet for positive experiences.

I stopped concentrating on what I didn't have yet. Suddenly, I found myself noticing the beauty in the every day: the warmth of the sun on my face, the laughter of loved ones, and the simple joy of waking up each morning. Everything changed for me.

I am even grateful for the cancer leading to my double mastectomy. The hard truth is that I wouldn't be here today to share my story if it was never found. This is how gratitude can help transform your mindset and help you continuously try and find the silver lining in almost every situation.

Thanks to gratitude, each of my days now begins and ends with a profound sense of appreciation. I silently express gratitude throughout the day for anything I notice—a blooming flower, a clear sky, or a friendly passerby. From my children texting me good morning to green lights all the way on my ride into work and even an order that comes in at the office—these are just a few of the many things I once took for granted. My days have become filled with moments of appreciation, and I've discovered that being thankful has painted my world with a comforting glow that brings me contentment. It has become natural and intuitive for me to be grateful for everything: the bad, the good, and the unknown of what is yet to come. I am now simply more attuned, actively and inherently seeking out these little joys. With this practice, I have become much happier, more fulfilled, and less irritable than before. My family and colleagues can attest to how miserable I could be, especially before my first cup of coffee.

I now trust that all will work out as it should.

Some ways you can practice gratitude.

1. Start Small: I encourage you to begin each day by identifying three simple things you are grateful for. These can be simple and basic things that are easy to see as good things.
2. Reflect on the Day: Before bed, take a few minutes to reflect on the positive aspects of your day. This could involve recalling moments of kindness, achievements, or even small victories.
3. Say Thank You: express gratitude verbally or in writing to those who have helped or positively impacted your day or life. This could be a simple thank-you note to a coworker, a heartfelt message to a family member, or a compliment to a stranger.
4. Practice Acts of Kindness: Engage in acts of kindness towards others. Perform small acts of kindness, such as holding the door for someone, offering a sincere compliment, or volunteering your time to help those in need.
5. Keep a Gratitude Jar: Create a gratitude jar and write down one thing you are grateful for each day on a small piece of paper. At the end of the week or month, empty the jar and read through the notes to remind yourself of the good things in your life.

By practicing gratitude, you can gradually train your mind to experience the positive effects on your overall well-being. Being thankful shifts our focus from what we lack to what we have. As the saying goes, **"Gratitude turns what we have into enough.**[10]**"** By acknowledging and appreciating the blessings already bestowed upon us, big and small, we invite more positivity and fulfillment into our existence.

---

[10] *Melody Beattie*

1. I am grateful for the gift of life and all its possibilities.

2. I appreciate the love and support of my friends and family.

3. Each day, I find new reasons to be grateful.

4. My heart overflows with gratitude for the beauty of nature.

5. I am grateful for the abundance that surrounds me.

6. Gratitude fills my heart and radiates from within me.

7. I am thankful for the simple joys.

8. I express gratitude for my body and its miraculous abilities.

9. I am grateful for the opportunities that come my way.

10. My past experiences, both good and bad, have shaped me, and I am thankful.

Chapter Fifteen

---◦◯◦---

Authenticity

Our second to last topic of discussion is another aspect called authenticity. Authenticity is like a GPS for an easy, happy life. When you're true to yourself, you navigate through challenges with honesty, freeing up mental space that would otherwise be spent on maintaining a facade.

Surround Yourself with the Right People

Embracing authenticity involves surrounding yourself with people and experiences that align with your true self. By doing so, you can create a life that is only achieved by eliminating the weight of pretending to be someone you are not, allowing joy to flow naturally. Think of it this way: do you feel more in tune with who you are and your goals when you are surrounded by people you love or people who make you feel bad about yourself? Be authentic in your interactions – surround yourself with people who make you *feel good*.

Genuine emotions back authentic intentions. The emotional energy you invest in your intentions amplifies their power. Authentic intentions remain consistent with your core values and beliefs. They don't waver with external influences, making them a stable and reliable force. The people who matter want to see and be with the real you. Being real helps you find your tribe. The people who will cheer you on, who understand, love, and accept you as you are.

Authentic Execution – "Be Real"

Being real is about being authentic. Authentic execution refers to taking actions that align with your true self. Such actions are more likely to bring you fulfillment and success. Pursuing your goals authentically requires passion and persistence, which are crucial qualities for overcoming obstacles and achieving goals. Authenticity also gives you the strength to persevere in the face of setbacks. Committing to your authentic path keeps you resilient and determined.

Moreover, embracing authenticity allows you to cultivate deeper connections and more meaningful relationships. When you show up authentically in your interactions with others, you attract genuine relationships and partnerships based on mutual respect and understanding. This authenticity fosters trust and authenticity in return, creating a support system of people who uplift and empower one another on their respective journeys.

My sisters, who are my best friends, are my biggest support system, and they love me for who I am- even **when I can be very hard to love**. They call me out on my bullsh*t and keep me grounded. They are there to listen and **to hold me accountable**. But they *always show up*, no matter how often they are leaned on. I trust them with my life; they have influenced my most significant decisions. The bond **transcends our bloodline**. There is real friendship and truth in our daily interactions.

By living authentically, you can create a life that reflects your true desires and values. This also allows you to remain consistent with your core values and beliefs. They don't waver with external influences, making them a stable and reliable force.

It is important to take time to reflect on your values, desires, and beliefs in order to understand what authenticity means to you. Ensure that your intentions align with your authentic self by engaging in self-reflection. Be honest about what you truly want. Authenticity often requires courage to break free from society's expectations and follow your heart's calling. Avoid compromising your authenticity for short-term gains.

Authenticity is not just a buzzword; it's the key to unlocking your full potential. When your intentions and actions are aligned with your authentic self, you create a powerful energy that resonates in the world around you. This resonance attracts the people, opportunities, and experiences that align with your desires. It is that simple.

Amidst the chaos in my own life, I've discovered that trying to be someone I'm not only leads to disappointment, frustration, and awkward situations. I've embraced my *hurricane personality* as my true self and remain unconcerned and undeterred by those expecting me to conform to some notion of "normal." Normal tends to be boring, and I would pretty much rather be just about almost anything else.

To those who find me "too much," "too loud," and "too big," those who believe I take up "too much space" with my big opinions and my bigger mouth—I say, "TOO BAD" because I refuse to diminish myself to fit into their narrow little minds and limited perceptions. I am unapologetically ME! I urge you to love all the unique parts of your personality as well.

It is totally freeing to be unbound and unbothered by others' expectations. I encourage you to embrace authenticity as your most potent tool. Let the real you shine its brightness into the world. You and your ideas have value. Let your ideas burn bright, glow outward, and inspire others.

1. I embrace my authentic self in all aspects of life.

2. My authenticity is my greatest source of power.

3. Authenticity is the cornerstone of my success.

4. I am unapologetically authentic in my actions.

5. I trust that my true self is more than enough.

6. I express my desires and intentions authentically.

7. I attract opportunities that align authentically.

8. Authenticity leads to clarity in my goals.

9. I release the fear of judgment.

10. My authenticity is a source of inspiration to others.

Chapter Sixteen

———•◦○◦•———

Laugh About It

All my life, I have used humor as a way to *protect myself*, in a way, from mean comments. I would crack a joke about my weight to take away the power of someone else doing it first. I bet if you ask any person who has ever been overweight, chances are they will have done the same thing at some point. It is as much of a form of self-preservation as it is a coping mechanism. When you're the *funny fat friend,* people don't see the point in making fun of you – you've already done it yourself. You're seen as amusing and carefree. If you're relaxed about it, others might be as well and steer away from it being a topic of discussion. We act like our feelings don't get hurt and that we don't care. But of course, deep down, we care. We really care. So, maybe we use humor as a defense mechanism. It's a tool. Humor diffuses. The upside here is that we usually hone humor into a killer skill, which becomes a great part of our personality.

By infusing humor into my narrative, I disarm the discomfort that typically accompanies such discussions about tough topics. I have found that sharing it this way aids in my own healing process and provides a sense of relatability to those with similar experiences. It also ensures that people listening understand that I am not sharing this part of my background to illicit pity or even empathy. In framing it lightly, it just becomes an informational reference or explanation of who I am and why I am the way I am. In a small way, it also challenges the stigma around discussing trauma and heavy topics openly. Through laughter and humor, I reclaim my story.

So, we shouldn't underestimate the role of laughter in our lives! It is a remedy that you can use daily. It's like having an ace up our sleeve, unlocking endorphins, lowering stress levels, and bringing a sprinkle of light into each day. Laughter can relax the entire body, relieving physical tension and stress and strengthening the immune system – something we all need as busy people in this fast-paced life! This is in addition to the bonus of boosting our air intake and working on our lungs and muscles. Next to eating chocolate, this is my favorite way to produce happy hormones!

Find Humor Where You Can

There are times in life when we are *really* down. It feels like things just won't be getting better anytime soon. These are the moments where you *need* to find the humor in the situation. I'm not saying that you should make light of the problem as though it's not even happening, as a form of denial. Nor should you use self-deprecating jokes (remember, the goal here is to be *positive)*. My advice is to focus on finding something funny about the situation. Try to find the silver lining. I have become a pro at finding humor in just about anything. Very few things are too sacred to be laughed about.

If you are struggling to find the humor in the situation, ask yourself, *what would someone else find funny in this situation?* Look for the absurd. Look for the silly or ridiculous. That's usually where the belly laughs come into play.

Of course, finding humor in certain situations will sometimes be hard. There are degrees of gravity to everything. Losing your home, losing someone close, or if you are financially struggling to make ends meet – some things are more complex than others to take lightly.

Do try to see the funny side of things when you can. It'll take off some of that heavy emotional load you're carrying. A good laugh, like a good cry, can be cathartic.

1. Humor lightens my burdens.

2. I see the silver lining in everything.

3. I love the sound of other people's laughter.

4. I have the power to make myself laugh.

5. My superpower is turning awkward moments into memorable jokes.

6. I am the director of my life, and sometimes it's a comedy.

7. I find joy in 'oops' moments because perfection is overrated and boring.

8. I see life's absurdities and laugh.

9. I'm finding comfort and humor in the simplest things.

10. My laughter is louder than my worries.

Conclusion

———•◉•———

We come to the end of our journey together, and you will now embark on a new one – a journey of continuing your *own* self-discovery and growth. I have aimed to pass along insights for you to weave into the fabric of your life, tailoring them to your personal aspirations and development. I am cheering you on as you dive deeper into understanding yourself and embark on the essential inner work for growth and healing.

Throughout our journey, you might have noticed themes echoing repeatedly. This is not a glitch in the matrix; instead, it's by design. The essence of cultivating a positive mindset and living a life that is filled with joy is deeply interwoven. Each puzzle piece interlocks to complete a mosaic, bringing the picture of all you desire into focus. Repetition reinforces these thoughts on both a conscious and subconscious level.

Choosing to explore these pages already marks a milestone in your journey. It's a testament to your willingness to grow, challenge the status quo, and embark on a quest for a more prosperous, more vibrant future! Your genuine curiosity signifies an open-minded disposition. It represents a remarkable stride towards positivity. Your simple action puts you miles ahead of others who don't choose to learn and grow.

Life, as we know, is not devoid of shadows. Negative thoughts, grief, doubt, fear, and sadness are all part of the emotional tapestry we navigate. Acknowledging and experiencing these emotions is not a sign of weakness but a part of our shared humanity. Consider reframing these emotions into positive opportunities for growth as they arise.

In my own trek, I've learned to let these emotions pass through fleetingly, not allowing them to anchor in my mind for too long, like clouds on a windy day. They can knock on my door and visit me, but I don't offer them a bed to sleep in. If this happens to you, let the feelings and emotions flow over and past you, placing them behind you as you gaze toward the future. Refrain from dwelling on anything that feels like it induces a lump in your throat. Such experiences are detrimental to your mind, heart, and soul. Never empower any aspect of your life to make you feel diminished or small. Focus on the positive path ahead, where resilience and strength reside.

Remember to treasure the simple moments, as they are the foundation on which the extraordinary is built. Keep positivity by your side as a constant companion, allowing it to brighten even the darkest moments on your path.

As you venture forward, embracing the practices shared in the previous chapters may help illuminate your path. Here's a short list of some of the tips explored to help make positivity a natural part of your day:

1. **Daily Rituals:** Kickstart your day with affirmations. Whether in bed, in front of a mirror, or during your commute, setting a positive tone first thing in the morning can work wonders.
2. **Written Words:** Jot down your affirmations. Plaster them on sticky notes or in a journal where they're always in view, constantly reminding you of your journey and progress.
3. **Visualization:** Pair your affirmations with vivid visualizations. Close your eyes and immerse yourself in the reality of your dreams, enhancing the power behind your intentions.
4. **Affirmation Cards:** Keep your favorite affirmations close at hand. Whether in your wallet or on your desk, let them be a quick source of inspiration and positivity.
5. **Tech Support:** Utilize apps for daily affirmations. They're a modern convenience that can seamlessly integrate positivity into your digital routine.

6. **Positive Spaces:** Cultivate an environment that echoes your goals. Surround yourself with motivational quotes and imagery that inspire your journey.

7. **Actionable Affirmations:** Apply your affirmations to real-life scenarios. Use them as a boost in moments that require an extra dose of confidence or strength.

8. **Mindful Moments:** Incorporate mindfulness or prayer to stay grounded. These practices not only reduce stress but connect you with your inner self, amplifying happiness.

9. **Grateful Heart:** Practice gratitude. Acknowledging the blessings you have attracts more positivity and abundance into your life. Being thankful for what you have already is key in this process. It is a real game-changer!

10. **Patience and Persistence:** Remember, transformation doesn't happen overnight. Be patient with yourself and stay committed to your practices, even when you don't see immediate results.

11. **Open Horizons:** Be receptive to new experiences and connections. Life's richness often lies beyond the comfort zone of our daily routines.

At this point, you have a good handle on the basic concepts that will help transform your life. Embark on this adventure with an open heart and mind.

As you go forward armed with these tools, remember that your thoughts are the seeds, your intentions are the compass, your gratitude is the fuel, and your authenticity is the true north guiding you to the abundant and authentic life you were born to live.

You are choosing to live your life to its fullest potential rather than just existing, which is a transformative decision. My own journey reflects this choice. In a career that fills me with joy and fulfillment, I've found that "work" feels more like a passion pursued daily. The thrill of learning, especially from the vibrant minds of younger colleagues, keeps me engaged and eager to face new challenges. It's a mutual exchange of inspiration, sparking healthier habits and a rejuvenated mindset. These new processes we've implemented save me loads of time and energy, affording me the freedom to explore new passions as I enjoy the new level of work-life balance.

Each day is an opportunity to explore new choices, and it's thrilling to sift through the possibilities. I make it a point to carve out time for reading, attending events, dining at great restaurants with family and friends, and indulging in self-care routines. Recently, I channeled my free time into creative pursuits, crafting a cookbook of generational Greek recipes, a children's book on our favorite holiday Easter traditions, and this very book, born from a series of positivity notes shared among friends. These projects, set to launch simultaneously over the next few weeks, are sure to mark the beginning of another exciting phase. Now, I find myself splitting my time between my homes on Long Island and Binghamton, NY, and the sunny, warm foothills of the Catalina mountains in Arizona.

I am considering accepting the offer to speak at a motivational event in Florida. It could be fun to participate in a brainstorming session. I am excited about the multiple vacations I've already booked—to revisit Italy and Greece, my favorite Mediterranean destinations. I cannot wait to go back this summer. Oh my God, the amazingly healthy and delicious Mediterranean food and those beaches! I am also eager to see the Northern Lights in Iceland in the fall and feel the warmth of the geothermal Blue Lagoon. I cannot wait to reap the benefits of the minerals in the warm waters and enjoy the luxury and relaxation of the amazing, planned trips. Where will I go next? My daughter mentioned Thailand and Japan, so those will likely end up on the itinerary. What new adventure awaits? The possibilities are endless, with remarkable things to do, see, try, revisit, and enjoy.

The coming year will indeed be a good kind of busy. Watching my children achieve great academic feats and incredible life milestones fills me with pride and deep fulfillment. Growing into their unique personalities and abilities, my nephews and niece bring joy to every day. My nephew got into the university of *his dreams*; we are also excited about his new adventure. His twin, a tiny *superhero*, continues to defy all odds, inspiring others with his determination and strong will. Despite being non-verbal, he communicates his wants and needs, consistently achieving what he sets his mind to. He walks and eats with gusto, contrary to every prognosis that he would be on a feeding tube and wheelchair-bound or that he wouldn't make it past his toddler years. My sister and her husband, refusing to give up on their son, have advocated for him at every turn. Seventeen years later, he remains a mischievous troublemaker, bringing out the best in everyone lucky to know him. Living proof that ordinary people can be remarkable just by existing!

My other sister has also defied the odds against the cancer that tried to ravage her, continuing to make us laugh, spoil her nieces and nephews, and spread her special brand of kindness and *mushy love* everywhere.

Life is good these days, **so good**. The old me would be waiting for the other shoe to drop, worried that things were **almost too good** and something would go wrong soon. But I've found an inner *calm and peace* that allows me to approach everything clearly. I make decisions confidently and feel safe and secure, knowing all will be well. I want **everyone** to *feel this way*.

My resilience, determination, willingness to adapt and grow, and new "*can do*" attitude are some of my favorite things about me. **What qualities do you love about yourself?** What are the **best things about you?** Take a moment to think about it and write it down before you start to doubt or let the little voice that says mean things have its way. *Lean into those good things*, good thoughts, and good feelings about yourself, and start your journey from *that place*.

May you always trust in the process and the journey. May you always believe in yourself and never lose sight of the boundless opportunities that await you. If you can think it, you can be it. Yes, **you can**.

A positive mindset is all the power you will ever need. The power of possibility is **always** inside **YOU**.

Now go live your best life.

Bonus
Additional Affirmations

"I Am" Affirmations

1. I am a vessel of creativity and innovation.
2. I am resilient in the face of adversity.
3. I am a source of joy and positivity.
4. I am a lifelong learner, constantly growing.
5. I am a leader in my community and circles.
6. I am loved for who I am.
7. I am a giver and receiver of love.
8. I am firm in my convictions and values.
9. I am a beacon of hope and inspiration.
10. I am a creator of my happiness.
11. I am in control of my destiny.
12. I am mindful and present in every moment.
13. I am a magnet for abundance and prosperity.
14. I am a source of kindness and compassion.
15. I am a channel for positive energy and healing.
16. I am a source of inspiration to those around me.
17. I am in tune with my inner desires.
18. I am a loving and supportive friend and family member.
19. I am aligned with my purpose and calling in life.
20. I am a source of laughter and joy to others.

"I Believe" Affirmations

1. I believe in my inner strength and resilience.

2. I believe in the boundless opportunities.

3. I believe in lasting happiness.

4. I believe in the beauty of my dreams.

5. I believe in the importance of self-care.

6. I believe in my ability to inspire and motivate.

7. I believe in finding joy in life's simple pleasures.

8. I believe in kindness and empathy.

9. I believe in the richness of my experiences.

10. I believe in the power of a positive outlook.

11. I believe in the wisdom of my intuition.

12. I believe in the power of forgiveness.

13. I believe in the abundance of the universe.

14. I believe in the beauty of diversity and unity.

15. I believe in the goodness of humanity.

16. I believe in the strength of my character.

17. I believe in the endless opportunities for growth.

18. I believe in the importance of self-expression.

19. I believe in the blessings of each new day.

20. I believe in the resilience of the human spirit.

"I Feel" Affirmations

1. I feel empowered to make positive changes.

2. I feel grateful for the abundance in my life.

3. I feel deeply connected to those around me.

4. I feel serenity amid chaos.

5. I feel the joy of living each day to the fullest.

6. I feel empathy towards others and myself.

7. I feel my heart open to endless love.

8. I feel confident.

9. I feel the strength of my inner peace.

10. I feel a sense of achievement.

11. I feel hope even in challenging times.

12. I feel the serenity of a peaceful mind.

13. I feel the love and support of my family.

14. I feel the clarity of my emotions guiding me.

15. I feel the grace of acceptance for what it is.

16. I feel the wisdom of my intuition guiding me.

17. I feel the creativity flowing through me.

18. I feel the resilience of my spirit.

19. I feel the lightness of letting go of negativity.

20. I feel the authenticity of my true self.

"I Speak" Affirmations

1. I speak with gentleness and understanding.

2. I speak my desires into existence.

3. I speak with the wisdom of experience.

4. I speak to build bridges.

5. I speak gratitude daily.

6. I speak with the intent to uplift others.

7. I speak assertively and with conviction.

8. I speak in alignment with my highest values.

9. I speak of success and progress.

10. I speak words that mirror my inner beauty.

11. I speak to create harmony in my relationships.

12. I speak of my dreams with unshakable faith.

13. I speak affirmations that fortify my spirit.

14. I speak with intention and purpose in every conversation.

15. I choose words that inspire and uplift those I speak to.

16. I express myself with clarity and conviction.

17. My words create a positive impact on the world.

18. I speak my intentions into existence with confidence.

19. I speak with compassion and understanding towards others.

20. My words are a force for positive change.

"I Hear" Affirmations

1. I hear the wisdom of my intuition speaking clearly.

2. I hear the gratitude in my heart for the beauty around me.

3. I hear my inner wisdom.

4. I hear the messages of growth and transformation.

5. I hear the beauty of life's intricate details.

6. I hear the inspiration that fuels my creativity.

7. I hear the reassurance of my inner strength.

8. I hear the symphony of possibilities.

9. I hear the melodies of peace and serenity.

10. I hear the encouragement to follow my dreams.

11. I hear my inner guidance.

12. I hear messages of love all around me.

13. I hear the beauty in the voices of those I love.

14. I hear the reassurance of my resilience.

15. I hear messages of hope and inspiration.

16. I hear the universe's call to live with purpose.

17. I hear the beauty of the world's diversity.

18. I hear the encouragement to follow my heart's desires.

19. I hear messages of love and connection.

20. I hear the truth of my own inner voice.

"I Write" Affirmations

1. My words hold the power to create my reality.

2. Writing bridges the gaps.

3. Through writing, I breathe life into dreams.

4. The ink flows with energy.

5. Writing helps me to clarify my goals.

6. My words are the building blocks.

7. Every word written is a declaration of my intentions.

8. Through writing, I become the author of my unique life story.

9. I write with ease.

10. My writing is a powerful tool for self-expression.

11. Through writing, thoughts transform.

12. I write with passion and with purpose.

13. The act of writing ignites a spark.

14. Trusting in the writing process brings my desires into existence.

15. Written words inspire positivity.

16. As I write, my creativity shines.

17. The pages of my journal hold the keys to my dreams.

18. Each written word is an affirmation of my intentions.

19. Writing is a process of turning thoughts into tangible reality.

20. My written goals form a clear roadmap to my desired destination.

Abundance Affirmations

1. I am surrounded by abundance and prosperity.

2. I am skilled in managing my finances effectively.

3. Wealth creation is a natural part of my life.

4. I am receiving wealth from multiple sources.

5. I embrace new avenues of income.

6. My hard work is attracting wealth.

7. I am grateful for my financial success.

8. I live a life of luxury and comfort.

9. My mindset is aligned with success.

10. I attract wealth effortlessly by following my passions.

11. I am in control of my financial future and prosperity.

12. I radiate an aura of abundance.

13. Money comes to me in unexpected ways.

14. I am open to receiving the abundance.

15. I am financially free and independent.

16. My wealth allows me to enjoy a life of fulfillment and happiness.

17. I am aligned with the energy of financial success.

18. My thoughts and actions are in harmony with wealth creation.

19. I am a money magnet, attracting riches effortlessly.

20. Wealth and prosperity are my birthright.

Self-Love Affirmations

1. I celebrate my strengths.

2. I am deserving of all the good that comes my way.

3. I am constantly evolving into a better version of myself.

4. I am a vessel for creativity and innovation.

5. I am grounded in my values and beliefs.

6. I am an example of resilience.

7. I am in perfect alignment with my true self.

8. I am a catalyst for positive change.

9. Love and beauty surround me.

10. I am a radiant expression of life.

11. I am guided by wisdom and intuition.

12. I am limitless in my potential to succeed.

13. I am filled with joy.

14. I am creative, and ideas flow to me quickly.

15. I embrace my uniqueness and individuality.

16. I am kind and gentle with myself in all situations.

17. I am an architect of my life's path.

18. I am at peace with myself.

19. I attract loving, supportive relationships.

20. I am a reservoir of self-compassion.

Love Affirmations

1. I am worthy of a love that is pure and unconditional.

2. I attract loving and supportive people into my life.

3. My relationships are filled with trust and affection.

4. Love surrounds me and fills my heart.

5. I am open to giving and receiving love without fear.

6. I am a loving and lovable person.

7. Love flows through me and touches everyone I meet.

8. I am grateful for the love that is present in my life.

9. My heart is open to possibilities.

10. Love is my natural state of being.

11. I attract people who appreciate me.

12. I am open to the beauty and joy of love.

13. Love flows effortlessly into my life.

14. I attract kindness.

15. I radiate love.

16. I release any past hurts and open myself to love again.

17. I am a source of love and inspiration to my partner.

18. My relationships are filled with trust.

19. I am deserving of a love that uplifts and fulfills me.

20. I am deeply connected to the love within me.

Healthy Eating Affirmations

1. I am grateful for the abundance of nutritious foods available.

2. I choose foods that fuel my body.

3. I release the need for emotional eating.

4. I find healthier coping methods.

5. My relationship with food is balanced.

6. I nourish my body with foods that support my health and well-being.

7. Healthy eating is an enjoyable part of my life.

8. I make mindful choices.

9. I choose foods that energize and sustain me throughout the day.

10. I release any guilt or shame associated with eating.

11. I am capable of making healthy choices.

12. I am becoming more in tune with my body's nutritional needs.

13. Healthy eating comes easily to me.

14. I embrace my body's signals.

15. My body thrives on wholesome food.

16. Unhealthy cravings dissolve.

17. I cherish my body, treating it with love.

18. Foods that fuel vitality are my preferred choice.

19. Emotional eating no longer holds power.

14. Each day, my relationship with food becomes more positive and balanced.

Sleep Affirmations

1. I am grateful for the healing power of sleep.

2. I sleep with ease.

3. I enter a state of deep relaxation.

4. I release all worries before bedtime.

5. Sleep is an easy and essential part of my life.

6. I am in harmony with my sleep rhythms.

7. My body knows how to relax.

8. My sleep is a time of renewal and healing.

9. I trust in my body's ability to sleep deeply.

10. Sleep is a gift I give to myself each night.

11. I am grateful for the comfort of my bed.

12. Sleep restores my body, mind, and spirit.

13. As I lay down, I create a cocoon of relaxation around myself.

14. I am enveloped in a sense of calmness.

15. With each passing moment, I move effortlessly into a serene dreamland.

16. My body and mind release tension, creating the perfect conditions for sleep.

17. I enjoy the quiet stillness of the night, allowing sleep to embrace me.

18. Every night, I let go of the outside world, entering a state of pure relaxation.

19. Sleep is a gentle transition into a realm of dreams and rejuvenation.

20. I am grateful for the quiet moments that lead me into a peaceful slumber.

Opportunity Affirmations

1. I welcome challenges as opportunities for growth.

2. Opportunities are drawn to my positive energy and mindset.

3. I attract incredible opportunities with ease.

4. I have the courage to pursue opportunities.

5. My intuition guides me.

6. I am worthy of the opportunities that come my way.

7. I am constantly expanding my horizons.

8. I am open to unexpected and life-changing opportunities.

9. I am a magnet for opportunities.

10. I create opportunities through my actions.

11. I attract opportunities.

12. I seize opportunity.

13. I am grateful for opportunities.

14. I radiate positivity.

15. My life is filled with exciting possibilities.

16. I am open to the limitless potential of every opportunity.

17. Opportunities are the steppingstones to my dreams.

18. I am a proactive seeker of new opportunities.

19. I am destined for greatness, and opportunities find me.

20. I am grateful for the abundance of opportunities in my life.

Gratitude Affirmations

1. Gratitude is my mindset.

2. I appreciate the abundance of love.

3. I am thankful for the present moment.

4. Gratitude is my daily practice.

5. I appreciate the freedom to pursue my dreams and passions.

6. Each breath I take is a reminder of the gift of life.

7. I am grateful for wisdom.

8. I find joy in expressing gratitude to others.

9. My heart is a reservoir of gratitude.

10. I am thankful for the support of mentors and guides on my journey.

11. I appreciate the abundance of opportunities for growth.

12. Gratitude is the key to unlocking a life of fulfillment.

13. I am thankful for the love that fills my heart.

14. Gratitude is a beacon of light in my life.

15. I appreciate the beauty of every sunrise and sunset.

16. I am grateful for the gift of laughter.

17. I express gratitude for the strength in me.

18. Gratitude is the foundation of my abundance.

19. I am thankful for the opportunity to learn and evolve.

20. Each moment is a treasure, and I am grateful for it.

Authenticity Affirmations

1. My authenticity radiates positive energy.

2. I honor my unique gifts and talents.

3. I am a magnet for abundance in my truth.

4. I am on an authentic path to abundance.

5. I am a beacon of authenticity.

6. My true self is powerful.

7. I am worthy of abundance just as I am.

8. I release the need to pretend or conform to others' expectations.

9. I trust that being myself is the key.

10. I attract abundance effortlessly.

11. Authenticity brings peace and harmony.

12. I am free to be my authentic self, no matter the circumstances.

13. My authenticity attracts opportunities beyond my wildest dreams.

14. I trust in the flow of abundance that authenticity creates.

15. I am open to receiving abundance in its most authentic form.

16. Authenticity empowers me to live a life of purpose and abundance.

17. I attract financial abundance by being true to myself.

18. Authenticity leads to inner peace.

19. I am confident in my authentic expression.

20. My authentic intentions manifest effortlessly.

Write Your Own Affirmations

Made in United States
North Haven, CT
27 February 2024

49301825R00070